THE COMPLETE BOOK
OF HOME BAKING

EDITORIAL
US Food Editor: Linda Venturoni
Food Editor: Rachel Blackmore
Editorial Assistant: Sheridan Packer
Editorial Coordinator: Margaret Kelly

RECIPE DEVELOPMENT
Sheryle Eastwood, Donna Hay, Anneka
Mitchell, Penelope Peel, Belinda Warn,
Loukie Werle

PHOTOGRAPHY
Ashley Mackevicius, Harm Mol, Yanto
Noerianto, Andy Payne, Warren Webb

STYLING
Wendy Berecry, Rosemary De Santis,
Carolyn Fienberg, Jacqui Hing, Michelle
Gorry, Anna Philips, Susie Smith

DESIGN AND PRODUCTION
Manager: Sheridan Carter
Layout: Lulu Dougherty
Finished Art: Stephen Joseph

Specially produced for Book Express, Inc.
Airport Business Center,
29 Kripes Road,
East Granby, Connecticut, USA.
By arrrangement with
J.B. Fairfax Press Pty Limited
A.C.N. 003 738 430

North American Direct Sales rights in this
edition are exclusive to Book Express, Inc.

Formatted by J.B. Fairfax Press Pty Limited
Printed by Toppan Printing Co, Singapore

JBFP 310 US
The Complete Book of Home Baking
Includes Index
ISBN 1 86343 149 7

PRINTED IN SINGAPORE

THE COMPLETE BOOK
OF HOME BAKING

A J.B. Fairfax Press Publication

CONTENTS

INTRODUCTION

The Complete Book of Home Baking *offers you a tempting selection of baked goods. There is something for every occasion: quickbreads for special afternoon treats or desserts; cakes, cookies and loaves that are perfect for feeding hungry children or for putting in lunch boxes; sweet and savory pies and pastries for main meals, snacks and desserts; delicious breads and pizzas that will have your family asking for more; and a special chapter of children's cakes that are sure to be a hit at your next birthday party for kids.*

Within the pages of this book you will find recipes for many old favorites such as Rich Chocolate Cake, Chocolate Eclairs, Shortbread Creams and Dundee Cake. There are also many of today's popular recipes, including Chocolate Mud Cake, Chocolate Chip Cookies, Country Pear Cake and Spicy Coconut Apple Twists. All are guaranteed to win you the compliments of family and friends.

The Complete Book of Home Baking *is a comprehensive and invaluable reference for every home cook.*

NOTE TO READERS

For consistent results when cooking, and especially when baking, it is important to weigh and measure ingredients accurately. In this book you will find that US Standard cup measures and metric weights and measurements have been given. As it is not practical to give exact conversions, it is important that you do not switch from one set of measures to another within a recipe.

All spoon and cup measures given in this book are level; flour is white all-purpose and sugar is white unless otherwise stated.

Greater variety in cake sizes has been achieved by the use of some cake pans that are 3 in/7.5 cm deep – twice the depth of most standard pans. A straight-sided ring cake pan and long bar pan have also been used. All are available at better homewares and specialty kitchenware stores. When preparing pans for baking, be sure to follow the recommendations given on page 235.

Can sizes vary between countries and manufacturers. You may find the quantities in this book are slightly different from what is available. Use the can size nearest to the suggested size in the recipe.

Where microwave instructions occur in this book, a microwave with a 650 watt output has been used. Wattage on domestic microwave ovens varies between 500 and 800, and it may be necessary to vary the cooking times slightly, depending on your oven.

SIMPLY CHOCOLATE

*For many, chocolate is a delicious
obsession. The Aztecs, who discovered it,
considered chocolate 'food of the gods'. In its
various forms — block chocolate, cocoa powder
and chocolate chips, grated, melted and
chopped — chocolate is one of the most
popular ingredients in cakes,
cookies and bars.*

Chocolate Mud Cake (page 10)

CHOCOLATE MUD CAKE

Makes a deep 8 in/20 cm round cake
Oven temperature 250°F, 120°C

1 cup/2 sticks/250 g butter, chopped

10 oz/315 g semi-sweet cooking chocolate

5 eggs, separated

3 tablespoons superfine sugar

¹/₄ cup/30 g self-rising flour, sifted

RICH CHOCOLATE SAUCE
6 oz/185 g semi-sweet cooking chocolate, broken into small pieces

¹/₄ cup/¹/₂ stick/60 g unsalted (sweet) butter

³/₄ cup/5¹/₂ oz superfine sugar

¹/₄ cup/45 g cocoa powder, sifted

¹/₃ cup/90 mL milk

¹/₃ cup/90 mL whipping cream

1   Place butter and chocolate in top of a double boiler set over simmering water. Heat, stirring constantly, until butter and chocolate are melted and smooth. Remove from heat and set aside to cool slightly.

2   Beat egg yolks and sugar into chocolate mixture. Then fold in flour.

3   Place egg whites in a large bowl and beat until stiff peaks form. Fold egg whites into chocolate mixture. Pour batter into a 3 in/7.5 cm deep, greased and lined 8 in/20 cm round cake pan or springform pan. Bake for 1¹/₄ hours or until cooked when tested with a skewer. Turn off heat and cool cake in oven with door ajar.

4   To make sauce, place chocolate and butter in top of a double boiler set over simmering water and heat, stirring constantly, until butter and chocolate are melted. Stir in sugar and cocoa powder and mix to combine. Add milk and cream and cook, stirring occasionally, for 5 minutes longer. Remove from heat. Pour sauce into a pitcher and set aside to cool. Serve with cake.

QUICK NUT FUDGE CAKE

Makes a deep 8 in/20 cm round cake
Oven temperature 350°F, 180°C

¹/₂ cup/1 stick/125 g butter or shortening, melted

1¹/₂ cups/250 g packed brown sugar

2 eggs, lightly beaten

1 teaspoon vanilla

¹/₄ cup/30 g cocoa powder, sifted

2 cups/250 g self-rising flour, sifted

¹/₂ cup/60 g chopped walnuts

CHOCOLATE BUTTER FROSTING
¹/₂ cup/1 stick/125 g butter, softened

4 oz/125 g semi-sweet cooking chocolate, melted and cooled

2 egg yolks

¹/₂ cup/75 g confectioners' sugar, sifted

1   Place butter or shortening, brown sugar, eggs and vanilla in a large mixing bowl and mix to combine. Stir in cocoa powder, flour and walnuts. Mix well to combine.

2   Spoon batter into a greased and lined 8 in/20 cm round cake pan or springform pan and bake for 35-40 minutes or until cake is cooked when tested with a skewer. Stand cake in pan for 5 minutes before turning onto a wire rack to cool.

3   To make frosting, place butter in a mixing bowl and beat until light and fluffy. Add chocolate, egg yolks and confectioners' sugar and beat until smooth. Spread frosting over cold cake.

Cook's tip: If self-rising flour is unavailable, substitute 2 cups all-purpose flour sifted with 1 teaspoon cream of tartar and ¹/₂ teaspoon baking soda.

Double Choc Cookies,
Quick Nut Fudge Cake

Double Choc Cookies

1　Place butter or shortening and sugar in a food processor and process until mixture is light and creamy. Add flour, self-rising flour, eggs and melted chocolate and process until smooth. Stir in chocolate chips.

2　Place spoonfuls of mixture on greased baking sheets and bake for 8-10 minutes or until firm. Stand on sheets for 5 minutes before transferring to wire racks to cool.

Makes 30
Oven temperature 350°F, 180°C

¹/₄ cup/¹/₂ stick/60 g butter or shortening, softened

¹/₄ cup/60 g superfine sugar

1¹/₄ cups/155 g flour

¹/₄ cup/30 g self-rising flour

2 eggs

6 oz/185 g milk chocolate, melted and cooled

6 oz/185 g semi-sweet chocolate chips

CHOCOLATE ROLL

Serves 8
Oven temperature 350°F, 180°C

5 eggs, separated

¹/₄ cup/60 g superfine sugar

4 oz/125 g semi-sweet cooking chocolate, melted and cooled

3 tablespoons flour, sifted with 3 tablespoons cocoa powder

CHOCOLATE FILLING
2 oz/60 g semi-sweet cooking chocolate

²/₃ cup/170 mL whipping cream

1 Place egg yolks and sugar in a mixing bowl and beat until mixture is thick and creamy. Beat in chocolate, then fold in flour mixture.

2 Place egg whites in a bowl and beat until stiff peaks form. Fold egg whites into chocolate mixture. Pour batter into a greased and lined 10¹/₂ x 12³/₄ in/26 x 32 cm jelly roll pan and bake for 12-15 minutes or until just firm. Turn onto a damp teatowel sprinkled with superfine sugar and roll up from the short end. Set aside to cool.

3 To make filling, place chocolate and cream in a small saucepan and cook over a low heat, stirring, until chocolate melts and mixture is well blended. Bring to the boil, remove from heat and set aside to cool completely. When cold, place in a mixing bowl set in crushed ice and beat until thick and creamy.

4 Unroll cake, spread with filling and reroll. Refrigerate until ready to serve. To serve, cut into slices.

CHOCOLATE COFFEE TUILES

Makes 25
Oven temperature 350°F, 180°C

2 egg whites

¹/₂ cup/100 g superfine sugar

¹/₂ teaspoon instant coffee powder dissolved in ¹/₂ teaspoon water

1 teaspoon vanilla

1 tablespoon cocoa powder

4 teaspoons milk

¹/₄ cup/¹/₂ stick/60 g butter, melted and cooled

1 Place egg whites in a bowl and beat until soft peaks form. Gradually add sugar, beating well after each addition, until mixture is glossy and sugar dissolved. Fold in coffee mixture, vanilla, cocoa powder, milk and butter.

2 Drop spoonfuls of mixture 4 in/10 cm apart onto a greased baking sheet and bake for 5 minutes or until edges are set. Remove from sheet and wrap each wafer around the handle of a wooden spoon. Allow to cool for 2 minutes or until set. Repeat with remaining mixture.

Cook's tip: Cook only one sheet of tuiles at a time and work quickly when molding, as they set very quickly. If the tuiles set before being molded, return them to the oven for 30 seconds to 1 minute so that they regain their pliability.

CHOCOLATE RUM AND RAISIN SQUARES

Makes 25 squares
Oven temperature 350°F, 180°C

1 cup/125 g self-rising flour, sifted

4 teaspoons cocoa powder, sifted

¹/₂ cup/100 g superfine sugar

³/₄ cup/75 g grated dry coconut

¹/₂ cup/75 g golden seedless raisins, chopped

¹/₂ cup/1 stick/125 g butter, melted

1 teaspoon rum extract

3 tablespoons grated semi-sweet cooking chocolate

CHOCOLATE FROSTING
1 cup/155 g confectioners' sugar

4 teaspoons cocoa powder

1 tablespoon/15 g butter, softened

1 tablespoon water

1   Place flour, cocoa powder, sugar, coconut and raisins in a large mixing bowl. Combine butter and rum extract, pour into dry ingredients and mix well.

2   Press mixture into a greased and lined 9 in/23 cm square cake pan and bake for 20-25 minutes or until firm. Remove from oven and allow to cool in pan.

3   To make frosting, sift confectioners' sugar and cocoa powder together into a mixing bowl. Add butter and water and beat to make a frosting of an easy-to-spread consistency.

4   Remove layer from pan and spread with frosting. Sprinkle with grated chocolate. Cover and refrigerate until frosting is firm. Cut into squares.

Cook's tip: If self-rising flour is unavailable substitute with 1 cup all-purpose flour sifted with ¹/₄ teaspoon baking soda.

RICH CHOCOLATE CAKE

1 Place butter or shortening and vanilla in a large mixing bowl and beat until light and fluffy. Gradually add sugar, beating well until mixture is light and creamy.

2 Beat in eggs, one at a time, then mix in chocolate. Sift together flour, baking powder and cocoa powder. Fold flour mixture and milk, alternately, into chocolate mixture.

3 Spoon cake batter into a 3 in/7.5 cm deep, greased and lined 8 in/20 cm round cake pan or springform pan and bake for 50-55 minutes, or until cooked when tested with a skewer. Stand in pan for 5 minutes before turning onto a wire rack to cool.

4 To make frosting, place butter in a bowl and beat until light and fluffy. Add chocolate, egg yolks and confectioners' sugar and beat until smooth.

5 Split cold cake in half horizontally. Spread bottom half of cake with jam and top with other half. Spread frosting over top and sides of cake.

Left: Chocolate Rum and Raisin Squares
Above: Rich Chocolate Cake

Makes a deep 8 in/20 cm round cake
Oven temperature 350°F, 180°C

$^3/_4$ cup/1$^1/_2$ sticks/185 g butter or shortening, softened

1 teaspoon vanilla

1$^1/_4$ cups/280 g superfine sugar

3 eggs

3 oz/90 g semi-sweet cooking chocolate, melted and cooled

1$^3/_4$ cups/220 g flour

2 teaspoons baking powder

$^1/_4$ cup/30 g cocoa powder

$^3/_4$ cup/185 mL milk

$^1/_3$ cup/100 g strawberry jam

CHOCOLATE BUTTER FROSTING
$^1/_2$ cup/1 stick/125 g butter, softened

4 oz/125 g semi-sweet cooking chocolate, melted and cooled

2 egg yolks

$^1/_2$ cup/75 g confectioners' sugar, sifted

CHESTNUT LOG

Serves 8

14 oz/440 g canned sweetened chestnut purée

$^1/_2$ cup/1 stick/125 g unsalted (sweet) butter, softened

1 egg

2-3 drops vanilla

$^1/_4$ cup/60 mL rum

24 purchased ladyfingers or make your own (see page 46)

CHOCOLATE GLAZE
3 tablespoons cocoa powder

4 teaspoons superfine sugar

3 tablespoons water

COFFEE FROSTING
$^3/_4$ cup/125 g confectioners' sugar

$^1/_2$ cup/1 stick/125 g unsalted (sweet) butter, softened

4 teaspoons coffee extract (chicory)

1 Place chestnut purée, butter, egg, vanilla and half the rum in a bowl and beat until smooth. Grease the bottom and sides of a $4^1/_2$ x $8^1/_2$ in/11 x 21 cm loaf pan and line with ladyfingers. Sprinkle ladyfingers with remaining rum. Spoon chestnut mixture into pan and top with remaining ladyfingers. Cover and refrigerate until firm.

2 Turn log onto a serving plate.

3 To make glaze, place cocoa, sugar and water in top of double boiler set over simmering water. Heat, stirring constantly, until sugar dissolves and glaze is smooth. Remove from heat and set aside to cool. Brush three-quarters of the glaze over log.

4 To make frosting, place confectioners' sugar, butter and coffee extract (chicory) in a bowl and beat until creamy. Spoon frosting into a pastry bag fitted with fluted tube and decorate log with rosettes of frosting. Drizzle remaining glaze over log.

Cook's tip: If coffee extract (chicory) is unavailable substitute 1 teaspoon instant coffee powder dissolved in 1 tablespoon hot water.

Above: Chocolate Eclairs
Left: Chestnut Log

CHOCOLATE ECLAIRS

Makes 8 éclairs
Oven temperature 425°F, 220°C

ECLAIR DOUGH
3 oz/90 g butter, chopped

1 cup/250 mL water

1 cup/125 g flour, sifted

4 eggs, lightly beaten

BRANDY CREAM FILLING
1¹/₂ cups/375 mL whipping cream

3 tablespoons confectioners' sugar

3 tablespoons brandy

CHOCOLATE TOPPING
5 oz/155 g semi-sweet cooking chocolate, melted

1 tablespoon/15 g butter, melted

1 To make éclairs, melt butter in a medium saucepan. Add water and bring to the boil over a medium heat. Add flour all at once and stir vigorously over heat until mixture leaves the sides of pan and forms a smooth ball. Transfer mixture to a bowl and set aside to cool for 10 minutes. Add eggs, one at a time, beating with a wooden spoon until smooth after each addition.

2 Spoon batter into a large pastry bag fitted with a ¹/₂ in/1 cm plain tube and pipe 4 in/10 cm lengths onto baking sheets lined with parchment paper. Bake for 10 minutes, reduce oven temperature to 350°F/180°C and bake for 25 minutes longer. Turn off heat and allow éclairs to cool with oven door open.

3 To make filling, place cream, confectioners' sugar and brandy in a bowl and whip until soft peaks form. Split éclairs lengthwise and fill with Brandy Cream Filling.

4 For topping, combine melted chocolate and butter and drizzle over top of éclairs.

CHOCOLATE PINWHEELS

Makes 30
Oven temperature 350°F, 180°C

**½ cup/1 stick/125 g butter or
shortening**

⅔ cup/140 g superfine sugar

1 teaspoon vanilla

1 egg

1¾ cups/220 g flour, sifted

¼ cup/30 g cocoa powder, sifted

1   Place butter or shortening, sugar and vanilla in a mixing bowl and beat until mixture is light and creamy. Add egg and beat until well combined.

2   Divide mixture into two equal portions and mix 1 cup/125 g of the flour into one portion and remaining flour and cocoa powder (sifted together) into the other portion.

3   Roll out each portion of dough between two sheets of waxed or parchment paper to form an 8 x 12 in/20 x 30 cm rectangle. Remove top sheet of paper from each and invert one layer onto the other. Roll up from longer edge to form a long roll. Wrap in plastic wrap and refrigerate for 1 hour.

4   Cut roll into ¼ in/5 mm slices and place on greased baking sheets. Bake for 10-12 minutes or until lightly browned. Cool on wire racks.

Cook's tip: These are ideal last-minute cookies. The dough can be made in advance and kept in the refrigerator or freezer until needed. Just slice the desired number of cookies off the roll and bake.

CHOCOLATE SHORTBREAD

Makes 30
Oven temperature 325°F, 160°C

1 cup/2 sticks/250 g butter, softened

½ cup/75 g confectioners' sugar

1 cup/125 g flour

1 cup/125 g cornstarch

¼ cup/30 g cocoa powder

1   Place butter and confectioners' sugar in a bowl and beat until mixture is creamy. Sift together flour, cornstarch and cocoa powder. Stir flour mixture into butter mixture.

2   Turn dough onto a lightly floured surface and knead lightly until smooth. Roll teaspoons of mixture into balls, place on greased baking sheets, flatten slightly with a fork and bake for 20-25 minutes or until firm. Allow to cool on sheets.

CHOCOLATE CHERRY STRUDEL

1 To make filling, place sour cream, brandy and sugar in a mixing bowl and beat until smooth and well combined. Stir in cherries.

2 Layer sheets of pastry, brushing every second sheet with butter and sprinkling with chocolate. Finish with a layer of chocolate.

3 Spoon filling down center of pastry. Fold in short ends, then starting from long end roll up. Place strudel seam side down on a well-greased baking sheet, brush with remaining butter and bake for 10 minutes. Reduce oven temperature to 350°F/ 180°C and bake for 20-30 minutes longer or until golden brown. Serve warm with whipped cream if desired.

Cook's tip: An easy way to grate chocolate is to use the food processor with the shredding disc. Place the chocolate in the feed tube and with machine running press down firmly on the chocolate.

Serves 10
Oven temperature 425°F, 220°C

8 sheets fillo (phyllo) pastry

1 tablespoon/15 g butter, melted

4 oz/125 g semi-sweet cooking chocolate, grated

CHERRY FILLING
1/2 cup/125 g dairy sour cream

2 teaspoons brandy

1 tablespoon granulated brown (raw or demerara) sugar

440 g/14 oz canned pitted tart red cherries, drained

CHOCOLATE FRUIT AND NUT BARS

1 Place almonds, hazelnuts (filberts), apricots, cherries, coconut, sugar and flour in a food processor and process to combine. With machine running, add chocolate and jam and process until ingredients are combined.

2 Press mixture into a shallow, greased and parchment paper -lined 7 x 11 in/18 x 28 cm cake pan and bake for 25-30 minutes or until firm. Set aside to cool in pan. Dust with confectioners' sugar and cut into bars.

Makes 25
Oven temperature 350°F, 180°C

1 cup/155 g almonds, chopped

3/4 cup/125 g hazelnuts (filberts), chopped

1 cup/125 g dried apricots, chopped

2/3 cup/125 g candied cherries, chopped

1 cup/90 g grated dry coconut

1/4 cup/60 g superfine sugar

1/4 cup/30 g flour

8 oz/250 g semi-sweet cooking chocolate, melted

1/4 cup/75 g apricot jam

confectioners' sugar

CHOCOLATE LAYER CAKE

Makes two 8 in/20 cm round layers
Oven temperature 350°F, 180°C

1 cup/125 g self-rising flour, sifted

¼ teaspoon baking soda

½ cup/45 g cocoa powder, sifted

½ cup/1 stick/125 g butter or shortening, softened

¾ cup/170 g superfine sugar

2 eggs, lightly beaten

1 cup/250 g dairy sour cream

½ cup/125 mL whipping cream, whipped

CHOCOLATE GLAZE
2 oz/60 g semi-sweet cooking chocolate, chopped

2 tablespoons/30 g unsalted (sweet) butter

1 Combine flour, baking soda, cocoa powder, butter or shortening, sugar, eggs and sour cream in a large mixing bowl and beat until mixture is smooth.

2 Spoon batter into two greased and floured 8 in/20 cm layer pans and bake for 25-30 minutes or until cooked when tested with a skewer. Stand cakes in pans for 5 minutes before turning onto wire racks to cool.

3 Spread one cake with whipped cream, then top with other cake.

4 To make glaze, place chocolate and butter in a small saucepan and cook over a low heat, stirring constantly, until melted. Cool slightly then spread over top of cake.

CHOCOLATE MERINGUE CAKE

1 To make meringue, place ground hazelnuts (filberts), cornstarch and ³/₄ cup/185 g sugar in a bowl and mix to combine.

2 Place egg whites in a bowl and beat until soft peaks form. Add remaining sugar a little at a time and beat until thick and glossy. Fold egg white mixture into hazelnut mixture.

3 Mark three 8 in/20 cm squares on parchment paper and place on baking sheets. Place meringue mixture into a pastry bag fitted with a small plain tube and pipe mixture to outline squares, then fill centers with piped lines of mixture. Bake for 40-50 minutes or until meringue is crisp and dry.

4 To make filling, place butter in a bowl and beat until soft. Add chocolate, superfine sugar and cream and beat until thick. Fold in brandy and hazelnuts (filberts). Set aside.

5 To make topping, place chocolate and oil in top of double boiler set over simmering water. Heat, stirring constantly, until chocolate melts and mixture is smooth. Remove from heat and set aside to cool.

6 To assemble cake, place a layer of meringue on a serving plate and spread with half the filling. Top with another meringue layer and remaining filling. Cut remaining meringue into smaller squares and position at angles on top of cake. Drizzle with topping and decorate with cream.

Serves 10
Oven temperature 250°F, 120°C

HAZELNUT MERINGUE
5 oz/155 g hazelnuts (filberts), ground

3 tablespoons cornstarch

1¼ cups/315 g sugar

6 egg whites

whipped cream

CHOCOLATE FILLING
³/₄ cup/1½ sticks/185 g unsalted (sweet) butter

6 oz/185 g semi-sweet cooking chocolate, melted and cooled

¼ cup/60 g superfine sugar

2 cups/500 mL whipping cream

3 tablespoons brandy

4 oz/125 g hazelnuts (filberts), ground

CHOCOLATE TOPPING
5 oz/155 g semi-sweet cooking chocolate

2 teaspoons vegetable oil

*Far left: Chocolate Layer Cake,
Chocolate Pinwheels (page 18)
Left: Chocolate Meringue Cake*

CHOCOLATE ALMOND BARS

Makes 18
Oven temperature 350°F, 180°C

1²/₃ cups/185 g slivered almonds,
coarsely chopped

²/₃ cup/75 g flour

2 eggs

¹/₃ cup/75 g superfine sugar

¹/₂ cup/170 g honey or light molasses

¹/₄ cup/60 mL melted butter

5 oz/155 g milk chocolate, melted

CHOCOLATE TOPPING
5 oz/155 g semi-sweet cooking
chocolate, melted

¹/₄ cup/¹/₂ stick/60 g butter, melted

1   Place almonds and flour in a bowl and mix to combine. Place eggs and sugar in a separate bowl and beat until light and fluffy, beat in honey or molasses, melted butter and chocolate. Stir egg mixture into almond mixture.

2   Pour batter into a shallow, greased and lined 7 x 11 in/18 x 28 cm cake pan and bake for 30 minutes or until firm. Stand in pan for 5 minutes before turning onto a wire rack to cool.

3   To make topping, combine chocolate and butter and spread over cold cake. Allow topping to set, then cut into bars, squares or diamonds.

WHITE CHOCO-CHIP CHOCOLATE CAKE

Makes a deep 9 in/23 cm round cake
Oven temperature 350°F, 180°C

¹/₂ cup/1 stick/125 g butter or
shortening, softened

1 cup/220 g superfine sugar

1 teaspoon vanilla

2 eggs

1¹/₃ cups/170 g self-rising flour

¹/₄ cup/30 g cocoa powder

¹/₂ teaspoon baking powder

1 cup/250 mL milk

6 oz/185 g white chocolate, chopped

WHITE CHOCOLATE FROSTING
¹/₂ cup/1 stick/125 g butter, softened

4 oz/125 g white chocolate, melted
and cooled

2 egg yolks

¹/₂ cup/75 g confectioners' sugar, sifted

1   Place butter or shortening, superfine sugar and vanilla in a bowl and beat until mixture is light and creamy. Add eggs one at a time, beating well after each addition.

2   Sift together flour, cocoa powder and baking powder. Fold flour mixture and milk, alternately, into butter mixture, then fold in white chocolate.

3   Spoon batter into a 3 in/7.5 cm deep, greased and lined 9 in/23 cm round cake pan or springform pan and bake for 30-35 minutes or until cooked when tested with a skewer. Stand in pan for 5 minutes before turning onto a wire rack to cool.

4   To make frosting, place butter in a bowl and beat until light and fluffy. Add chocolate, egg yolks and confectioners' sugar and beat until smooth. Spread frosting over top and sides of cake.

Cook's tip: If self-rising flour is unavailable, substitute with 1¹/₃ cups/170 g all-purpose flour sifted with ¹/₂ teaspoon cream of tartar and ¹/₄ teaspoon baking soda.

JAFFA PECAN CUPCAKES

1 Place chopped chocolate and butter or shortening in top of a double boiler set over simmering water. Heat, stirring constantly, until chocolate and butter melt and mixture is combined. Remove from heat and set aside to cool slightly.

2 Stir eggs, liqueur, orange rind, sugar and pecans into chocolate mixture and mix to combine. Fold in flour.

3 Spoon batter into muffin pan lined with paper bake cups, top with half a pecan and bake for 20 minutes or until cakes are cooked when tested with a skewer. Remove cakes from pan and allow to cool on wire rack.

4 Drizzle melted chocolate over cakes and allow to set.

Cook's tip: You can replace the orange-flavored liqueur with fresh orange juice if you wish.

Makes 12-14 cupcakes
Oven temperature 350°F, 180°C

4 oz/125 g semi-sweet cooking chocolate, chopped

1/2 cup/1 stick/125 g butter or shortening

2 eggs, beaten

3 tablespoons orange-flavored liqueur

2 teaspoons finely grated orange rind

3/4 cup/170 g/5 1/2 oz superfine sugar

2 oz/60 g pecans, chopped

1/2 cup/60 g flour, sifted

18 pecan halves

1 oz/30 g semi-sweet cooking chocolate, melted

CHOCOLATE FUDGE TORTE

1 Place butter or shortening and sugar in a bowl and beat until light and fluffy. Add egg yolks one at a time, beating well after each addition. Beat in melted chocolate and brandy, then fold in almonds and bread crumbs.

2 Place egg whites in a separate bowl and beat until stiff peaks form. Fold egg white mixture into chocolate mixture. Spoon batter into a 3 in/7.5 cm deep, greased and lined 9 in/23 cm springform pan and bake for 30-35 minutes or until cake is firm. Remove cake from pan and cool on a wire rack.

3 To make topping, place chocolate, corn syrup, butter and cream in a small saucepan and cook over a low heat, stirring constantly, until all ingredients are melted and combined. Spread topping over cold cake.

Makes a deep 9 in/23 cm round cake
Oven temperature 350°F, 180°C

1/3 cup/90 g butter or shortening

2/3 cup/155 g superfine sugar

5 eggs, separated

3 oz/90 g semi-sweet cooking chocolate, melted and cooled

3 tablespoons brandy

3/4 cup/90 g ground almonds

3/4 cup/45 g fresh bread crumbs

CHOCOLATE TOPPING
4 oz/125 g semi-sweet cooking chocolate, melted

3 tablespoons light or dark corn syrup

1 tablespoon melted butter

1 tablespoon whipping cream

CHOCOLATE MOCHA CAKE

Makes a deep 8 in/20 cm round cake
Oven temperature 325°F, 160°C

6 oz/185 g semi-sweet cooking chocolate, broken into small pieces

4 eggs, separated

¹/₂ cup/100 g superfine sugar

³/₄ cup/1¹/₂ sticks/185 g unsalted (sweet) butter, softened and cut into pieces

3 tablespoons strong black coffee

¹/₂ cup/60 g flour, sifted

CHOCOLATE GLAZE
6 oz/185 g semi-sweet cooking chocolate, broken into small pieces

¹/₃ cup/90 g unsalted (sweet) butter

2 tablespoons water

1   Place chocolate in top of a double boiler set over simmering water and heat, stirring occasionally, until chocolate melts. Remove from heat and stir until smooth. Set aside to cool.

2   Place egg yolks and sugar in a bowl and beat until light and fluffy. Add butter and beat until mixture is creamy. Add coffee and chocolate and continue beating until mixture is once again creamy. Sift flour over chocolate mixture and fold in lightly.

3   Place egg whites in a bowl and beat until soft peaks form. Fold egg white mixture into chocolate mixture. Pour batter into a 3 in/7.5 cm deep, greased and lined 8 in/20 cm round cake pan or springform pan and bake for 30 minutes, or until firm to touch. Turn off heat and cool cake in oven with door ajar. Turn cake out and refrigerate for 2 hours or overnight.

4   To make glaze, place chocolate, butter and water in top of a double boiler set over simmering water and heat, stirring constantly, until chocolate and butter melt. Remove from heat. Set aside to cool.

5   Remove cake from refrigerator and place on a wire rack. Place rack on a baking sheet and pour glaze over cake, smoothing it over edges and onto sides with a spatula. Leave until completely set. Transfer cake to a flat serving platter and cut into slices to serve.

Variation: For chocoholics this cake can be made even more special if you make two cakes, then sandwich them together with whipped cream and decorate the top of the cake with Chocolate Curls (Caraques, see page 226), or chocolate leaves.

Top: Chocolate Mocha Cake
Bottom: Devil's Food Cream Cake (page 26)

DEVIL'S FOOD CREAM CAKE

Makes three 9 in/23 cm round layers
Oven temperature 350°F, 180°C

1 cup/100 g cocoa powder

1¹/₂ cups/375 mL boiling water

1¹/₂ cups/3 sticks/375 g unsalted (sweet) butter, softened

1 teaspoon vanilla

1¹/₂ cups/315 g superfine sugar

4 eggs

2¹/₂ cups/315 g flour

¹/₂ cup/60 g cornstarch

1 teaspoon baking soda

1 teaspoon salt

¹/₂ cup/125 mL whipping cream, whipped

CHOCOLATE BUTTER FROSTING
1 cup/2 sticks/250 g butter, softened

1 egg

2 egg yolks

1 cup/155 g confectioners' sugar, sifted

6 oz/185 g semi-sweet cooking chocolate, melted and cooled

1   Place cocoa powder and water in a small bowl and mix until blended. Set aside to cool. Place butter and vanilla in a large mixing bowl and beat until light and fluffy. Gradually add sugar, beating well until mixture is creamy. Beat in eggs one at a time, beating well after each addition.

2   Sift together flour, cornstarch, baking soda and salt into a bowl. Fold flour mixture and cocoa mixture, alternately, into egg mixture.

3   Divide batter between three greased and floured 9 in/23 cm layer pans and bake for 20-25 minutes or until cakes are cooked when tested with a skewer. Stand cakes in pans for 5 minutes before turning onto wire racks to cool.

4   To make frosting, place butter in a mixing bowl and beat until light and fluffy. Mix in egg, egg yolks and confectioners' sugar. Add chocolate and beat until frosting is thick and creamy. Spread one cake with half the whipped cream, top with a second cake and spread with remaining whipped cream. Finally top with remaining cake and cover top and sides of cake with frosting.

BROWNIES

Makes 25
Oven temperature 350°F, 180°C

5 oz/155 g butter, softened

¹/₂ cup/170 g honey, warmed

1 tablespoon water

2 eggs, lightly beaten

1³/₄ cups/220 g self-rising flour, sifted

²/₃ cup/100 g packed brown sugar

4 oz/125 g semi-sweet cooking chocolate, melted and cooled

confectioners' sugar, sifted

1   Place butter, honey, water, eggs, flour, brown sugar and chocolate in a food processor and process until ingredients are combined.

2   Spoon batter into a greased and floured 9 in/23 cm square cake pan and bake for 30-35 minutes or until cooked when tested with a skewer. Stand cake in pan for 5 minutes before turning onto a wire rack to cool. Dust with confectioners' sugar and cut into squares.

Cook's tip: Chocolate can be melted quickly and easily in the microwave. Place 4 oz/125 g chocolate in a microwave-safe glass or ceramic dish and melt on HIGH (100%) for 1 minute. When melting chocolate in the microwave you will find that it tends to hold its shape, so always stir it before additional heating. If the chocolate is not completely melted, heat for 30 seconds longer, then stir again.

CHOCOLATE LOG

Serves 10
Oven temperature 325°F, 160°C

³/₄ cup/1¹/₂ sticks/185 g butter or shortening

¹/₄ cup/30 g cocoa powder

1 cup/250 mL hot water

6 oz/185 g semi-sweet cooking chocolate, chopped

1 cup/220 g superfine sugar

4 oz/125 g ricotta cheese

³/₄ cup/90 g flour

1 cup/125 g self-rising flour

2 eggs

CHOCOLATE FILLING
6 oz/185 g milk chocolate, melted

3 tablespoons whipping cream

¹/₂ cup/60 g chopped nuts

CHOCOLATE GLAZE
4 oz/125 g semi-sweet cooking chocolate

2 tablespoons/30 g butter

1 Place butter or shortening, cocoa powder, water, chocolate and sugar in a saucepan and cook over a medium heat, stirring constantly, until chocolate melts and ingredients are combined.

2 Transfer chocolate mixture to a large bowl. Beat in ricotta cheese, flour, self-rising flour and eggs. Continue beating until mixture is smooth. Spoon batter into a greased and lined 4¹/₂ x 8¹/₂ in/11 x 21 cm loaf pan and bake for 1¹/₂ hours or until cake is cooked when tested with a skewer. Allow cake to stand in pan for 5 minutes before turning onto a wire rack to cool.

3 To make filling, place chocolate, cream and nuts in a bowl and mix to combine. Cut cake horizontally into three layers. Spread two of the layers with filling, place one on top of the other, then top with plain layer.

4 To make glaze, place chocolate and butter in top of a double boiler set over simmering water and heat, stirring, until chocolate melts and mixture is smooth. Spread top and sides of cake with glaze and refrigerate until set.

CHOCOLATE LACE WAFERS

Makes 20
Oven temperature 350°F, 180°C

¹/₄ cup/90 g honey or light molasses

¹/₃ cup/90 g butter

¹/₃ cup/60 g packed brown sugar

¹/₂ cup/60 g flour

2 teaspoons cocoa powder

4 oz/125 g semi-sweet cooking chocolate, melted

1 Place honey or molasses, butter and sugar in a saucepan and cook over a medium heat, stirring constantly, until butter melts. Do not allow to boil. Stir in flour and cocoa powder.

2 Making 3 or 4 wafers at a time, drop teaspoons of mixture about 6 in/15 cm apart onto a greased baking sheet and bake for 5 minutes.

3 Allow wafers to stand on sheet for 1 minute, then remove using a spatula and lay over a rolling pin. Set aside to cool. Repeat with remaining mixture. Drizzle cold wafers with melted chocolate.

CHOCOLATE BROWNIE TORTE

Makes an 8 in/20 cm round cake
Oven temperature 350°F, 180°C

3 tablespoons/45 g butter, chopped

6 oz/185 g semi-sweet cooking chocolate, coarsely chopped

1 egg

¹/₄ cup/60 g superfine sugar

¹/₂ teaspoon vanilla

¹/₄ cup/30 g flour

¹/₂ cup/60 g slivered almonds

1 Place butter and 4 oz/125 g of the chocolate in top of a double boiler set over simmering water and heat, stirring, for 5 minutes or until chocolate melts and mixture is smooth. Remove from heat.

2 Place egg, sugar and vanilla in a bowl and beat until mixture is thick and creamy. Beat in chocolate mixture, then fold in flour, almonds and remaining chocolate. Spoon batter into a lightly greased and lined 8 in/20 cm layer pan and bake for 15-20 minutes or until cooked when tested with a skewer. Turn onto a wire rack to cool for 5-10 minutes before serving.

Serving suggestion: Cut torte into wedges and serve warm with a scoop of ice cream – coffee-flavored ice cream is a delicious accompaniment for this dessert.

BLACK FOREST GATEAU

Makes two 8 in/20 cm round layers
Oven temperature 350°F, 180°C

4 teaspoons cider vinegar

1 cup/250 mL evaporated milk

1¹/₂ cups/185 g flour

pinch salt

¹/₂ cup/45 g cocoa powder

1¹/₂ teaspoons baking soda

1¹/₄ cups/280 g superfine sugar

³/₄ cup/1¹/₂ sticks/185 g butter, melted

1 teaspoon vanilla

2 eggs, lightly beaten

CHERRY FILLING
20 oz/600 g canned pitted tart red cherries

2 tablespoons sugar

¹/₃ cup/90 mL cherry-flavored liqueur

2¹/₂ cups/600 mL whipping cream

¹/₄ cup/60 g superfine sugar

DECORATION
8 oz/250 g semi-sweet cooking chocolate, grated

¹/₂ cup/125 mL whipping cream, whipped

maraschino or candied cherries

1 Place vinegar and milk in a bowl and set aside.

2 Sift flour, salt, cocoa powder, baking soda and sugar together into a bowl. Pour in melted butter and half the milk mixture and beat for 2 minutes.

3 Add vanilla, eggs and remaining milk mixture and beat for 2 minutes longer. Spoon batter into two greased and lined 8 in/20 cm layer pans and bake for 35 minutes or until cakes are cooked when tested with a skewer. Allow cakes to cool in pans.

4 To make filling, drain cherries and reserve liquid. Measure ¹/₂ cup/125 mL reserved cherry liquid. Place cherry liquid, sugar and cherry-flavored liqueur in a small saucepan, bring to the boil, then reduce heat and simmer for 3 minutes. Remove pan from heat and set aside to cool. Place cream and sugar in bowl and beat until soft peaks form.

5 To assemble gâteau, split each layer horizontally. Place one cake half on a serving plate, brush liberally with cherry syrup, top with 8 tablespoons whipped cream, scatter with one-third of the cherries and finally top with another cake half. Repeat layers ending with a layer of cake. Brush top of cake with cherry syrup, then spread whipped cream over top and sides of cake.

6 To decorate, press grated chocolate onto top and sides of cake. Spoon remaining whipped cream in a pastry bag fitted with a fluted tube and pipe rosettes of cream around edge of cake. Place a maraschino cherry in the center of each rosette and chill cake for several hours before serving.

Chocolate Brownie Torte

MOCHA SPONGE

Makes two 7 in/18 cm layers
Oven temperature 375°F, 190°C

3 eggs, separated

¹/₂ cup/100 g superfine sugar

³/₄ cup/90 g self-rising flour

pinch salt

4 teaspoons cocoa powder

1 teaspoon melted butter

1 teaspoon instant coffee powder

2 tablespoons boiling water

COFFEE CREAM FILLING
4 teaspoons instant coffee powder

1 tablespoon hot milk

¹/₂ cup/125 mL whipping cream, whipped

1-2 tablespoons confectioners' sugar, sifted

FEATHERED GLAZE
1 cup/155 g confectioners' sugar, sifted

1 tablespoon boiling water

1 tablespoon/15 g butter

¹/₄ teaspoon vanilla

1 tablespoon caramel ice cream topping (sauce)

2 teaspoons instant coffee powder

1 Place egg whites in a bowl and beat until stiff peaks form. Gradually add sugar, beating well after each addition, until mixture is thick and glossy. Add egg yolks one at a time, beating well after each addition.

2 Sift together flour, salt and cocoa powder, then sift mixture twice more. Fold flour mixture into egg mixture. Combine butter, instant coffee powder and boiling water and pour around the edge of the batter, then lightly fold in.

3 Pour batter into two greased and lined 7 in/18 cm layer pans and bake for 20-25 minutes or until sponge springs back when touched with the fingertips. Allow cakes to stand in pans for 3-4 minutes before turning onto wire racks to cool.

4 To make filling, dissolve instant coffee powder in milk and fold into whipped cream. Sweeten to taste with confectioners' sugar. Spread one cake with filling, then top with other cake.

5 To make glaze, place confectioners' sugar in top of a double boiler and set over simmering water. Make a well in the center of the confectioners' sugar, add boiling water, butter and vanilla and cook, stirring slowly, until mixture is smooth and shiny. Pour half the mixture into a separate bowl and stir in the caramel topping (sauce). Stir instant coffee powder into remaining mixture.

6 Spread top of cake with caramel-flavored glaze. Then, while the glaze is still warm, place the coffee-flavored glaze in a plastic bag, snip off the corner and pipe parallel lines, ³/₄ in/2 cm apart, across the top of the cake. Using a metal skewer, lightly draw across the lines at ³/₄ in/2 cm intervals in the opposite direction, to give a feathered effect.

Cook's tip: When making a sponge cake, sift the dry ingredients three times to incorporate as much air as possible into the mixture. This helps to ensure a light-as-air cake.

FLORENTINE SQUARES

1 Place raisins, corn flakes, almonds, cherries and condensed milk in a large bowl and mix well to combine.

2 Spoon mixture into a greased and lined 9 in/23 cm square cake pan. Press down firmly using a fork and bake for 25-30 minutes or until firm. Stand in pan for 5 minutes before turning onto a wire rack to cool.

3 Cut into squares, then dip one corner of each square in melted chocolate. Set aside on a sheet of aluminum foil until chocolate sets.

Makes 30
Oven temperature 325°F, 160°C

³/₄ cup/125 g golden seedless raisins, finely chopped

2 cups/90 g corn flakes, crushed

³/₄ cup/90 g slivered almonds, toasted

¹/₂ cup/90 g candied cherries, chopped

²/₃ cup/170 mL sweetened condensed milk

4 oz/125 g semi-sweet cooking chocolate melted

CHOCOLATE SIENNA CAKE

1 Place macadamia or brazil nuts, walnuts, almonds, dates, raisins, coconut, flour, cocoa powder and confectioners' sugar in a bowl and mix to combine.

2 Place chocolate, butter and apricot jam in a saucepan and cook over a low heat, stirring, until ingredients are melted and combined. Pour chocolate mixture into fruit mixture and mix.

3 Spoon mixture into a greased and lined 9 in/23 cm round cake pan, pressing down firmly, and bake for 35 minutes. Stand cake in pan for 5 minutes before turning onto a wire rack to cool.

Cook's tip: Native to Australia the macadamia nut has a very hard shell and a delicious rich buttery flavor. In most recipes that call for macadamia nuts, brazil nuts can be used instead.

Makes a 9 in/23 cm round cake
Oven temperature 350°F, 180°C

2 oz/60 g macadamia or brazil nuts, chopped

1¹/₄ cups/125 g walnuts, chopped

³/₄ cup/125 g almonds, chopped

1 cup/155 g pitted dried dates, chopped

1 cup/170 g golden seedless raisins

¹/₃ cup/30 g grated dry coconut

¹/₂ cup/60 g flour

¹/₂ cup/45 g cocoa powder

¹/₂ cup/75 g confectioners' sugar

8 oz/250 g milk chocolate, grated

¹/₄ cup/¹/₂ stick/60 g butter

¹/₂ cup/155 g apricot jam

CAKES AND COOKIES FOR EVERY DAY

Your family and friends will be
delighted when you offer a tray of fresh cake or
open a cookie jar that actually contains
homemade cookies or bars. The recipes
in this chapter are great for morning and
afternoon coffee breaks and are equally as good
in packed lunches.

Victoria Sponge Cake (page 34), Eccles Cakes (page 35),
Chocolate Chip Cookies (page 34), Apricot Banana Loaf (page 35)

VICTORIA SPONGE CAKE

Makes two 8 in/20 cm round layers
Oven temperature 350°F, 180°C

4 eggs

³/₄ cup/170 g superfine sugar

1 cup/125 g self-rising flour

1 tablespoon cornstarch

¹/₃ cup/90 mL warm water

1¹/₂ teaspoons melted butter

1 tablespoon confectioners' sugar, sifted

FILLING

¹/₂ cup/155 g strawberry jam

¹/₂ cup/125 mL whipping cream, whipped

1　Place eggs in a large bowl and beat until thick and creamy. Gradually add sugar, beating well after each addition. Continue beating until mixture is very thick and creamy. This will take about 10 minutes.

2　Sift together flour and cornstarch over egg mixture and fold in. Stir in water and melted butter.

3　Divide mixture evenly between two greased and lined 8 in/20 cm layer pans. Bake for 20-25 minutes or until cake shrinks slightly from sides of cake pan and springs back when touched with the fingertips. Stand in pans for 5 minutes before turning onto a wire rack to cool.

4　To assemble, spread one sponge cake with jam, then top with whipped cream and remaining sponge cake. Sprinkle top of cake with confectioners' sugar and serve.

Passion Fruit Sponge Cake: Spread one sponge cake with lemon curd, then top with whipped cream and remaining sponge cake. Spread top of cake with passion fruit glaze. To make passion fruit glaze, combine 1 tablespoon/15 g softened butter and ¹/₄ cup/60 mL passion fruit pulp with 1 cup/155 g confectioners' sugar, sifted, and mix with enough water to make a glaze of an easy to spread consistency.

CHOCOLATE CHIP COOKIES

Makes 40
Oven temperature 400°F, 200°C

1 cup/2 sticks/250 g butter or shortening, softened

2 teaspoons vanilla

2 cups/350 g packed brown sugar

2 eggs

2 cups/250 g flour, sifted

1 cup/125 g self-rising flour, sifted

2 cups/185 g grated dry coconut

8 oz/250 g semi-sweet chocolate chips

1　Place butter or shortening, vanilla and sugar in a mixing bowl and beat until light and fluffy. Add eggs one at a time, beating well after each addition.

2　Stir in flour, self-rising flour, coconut and chocolate chips. Roll heaped spoonfuls of mixture into balls, place on well-greased baking sheets and flatten slightly. Bake for 12-15 minutes. Remove from oven and allow to stand on sheets for a few minutes before transferring to wire racks to cool.

ECCLES CAKES

1 To make filling, place sugar and butter in a saucepan and cook over a low heat, stirring, until butter melts. Stir in currants, mixed peel, allspice and nutmeg and cook for 2-3 minutes longer. Remove pan from heat and set aside to cool.

2 Roll pastry out to ¹/₈ in/3 mm thick. Using a 4 in/10 cm cutter, cut out rounds. Place a teaspoon of fruit mixture in center of each pastry round. Fold pastry over filling and pinch edges together. Turn rounds over so edges are facing downwards and flatten each cake gently using a rolling pin.

3 Make a small hole in the top of each cake. Combine sugar, nutmeg and allspice and sprinkle over cakes. Place on a greased baking sheet and bake for 12-15 minutes, or until pastry is golden and cooked. Remove from oven and place on wire racks to cool.

Makes 16
Oven temperature 425°F, 220°C

favorite pastry for a 2-crust pie

1 tablespoon superfine sugar

pinch ground nutmeg

pinch ground allspice

FRUIT FILLING
¹/₄ cup/60 g superfine sugar

2 tablespoons/30 g butter

³/₄ cup/125 g currants

3 tablespoons diced mixed candied citrus peel

¹/₂ teaspoon ground allspice

¹/₂ teaspoon ground nutmeg

APRICOT BANANA LOAF

1 Place butter or shortening in a bowl and beat until light and fluffy. Gradually add sugar, beating well until mixture is light and creamy.

2 Beat in egg, then mix in bananas. Sift together self-rising flour, wholewheat flour, baking soda, cream of tartar, cardamom, nutmeg and allspice into a bowl. Return grits to mixture. Fold flour mixture and milk alternately into banana mixture, then mix in apricots and pecans.

3 Spoon batter into a greased and floured 4¹/₂ x 8¹/₂ in/ 11 x 21 cm loaf pan and bake for 1¹/₄ hours or until cooked when tested with a skewer. Stand in pan for 5 minutes before turning onto a wire rack to cool.

Makes a 4¹/₂ x 8¹/₂ in/11 x 21 cm loaf
Oven temperature 350°F, 180°C

¹/₂ cup/1 stick/125 g butter or shortening, softened

1 cup/250 g sugar

1 egg

3 ripe bananas, mashed

1 cup/125 g self-rising flour

1 cup/155 g wholewheat flour

1¹/₄ teaspoons baking soda

¹/₂ teaspoon cream of tartar

1 teaspoon ground cardamom

¹/₂ teaspoon ground nutmeg

¹/₂ teaspoon ground allspice

¹/₂ cup/125 mL milk

1¹/₄ cups/155 g dried apricots, chopped

¹/₂ cup/90 g pecans, chopped

GINGERBREAD APRICOT UPSIDE DOWN CAKE

Makes an 8 in/20 cm ring cake
Oven temperature 350°F, 180°C

¹/₂ cup/60 g dried apricots

¹/₄ cup/¹/₂ stick/60 g butter or shortening, softened

¹/₂ cup/90 g packed brown sugar

¹/₃ cup/90 mL chopped pecans

GINGERBREAD CAKE
1 cup/125 g flour, sifted

¹/₂ cup/60 g self-rising flour, sifted

¹/₂ teaspoon baking soda

1 tablespoon ground ginger

¹/₂ teaspoon ground nutmeg

¹/₂ cup/90 g packed brown sugar

¹/₂ cup/170 g light molasses

¹/₂ cup/125 mL water

¹/₂ cup/1 stick/125 g butter

1   Place apricots in a bowl. Pour over boiling water to cover and soak for 30 minutes. Drain and set aside. Place butter or shortening and sugar in small bowl and beat until smooth. Spread mixture over bottom of a 3 in/7.5 cm deep, greased and lined 8 in/20 cm straight-sided ring pan. Sprinkle with pecans and top with apricots, cut side up.

2   To make cake, place flour, self-rising flour, baking soda, ginger, nutmeg and sugar in a large bowl. Place molasses, water and butter in a saucepan and cook over a low heat, stirring, until butter melts. Remove from heat and cool slightly. Pour molasses mixture into dry ingredients and stir until combined. Spoon batter into prepared pan and bake for 35-40 minutes. Stand in pan for 15 minutes before turning onto a wire rack to cool.

Cook's tip: Recipe can be baked in an 8 in/20 cm greased and parchment paper-lined springform pan if desired.

Below: Gingerbread Apricot Upside Down Cake,
Fruit Mincemeat Shortcake (page 38),
Right: Coconut Cake (page 38), Orange Coconut Loaf (page 39),
Oaty Choc-Chip Cookies (page 39)

FRUIT MINCEMEAT SHORTCAKE

Makes an 8 in/20 cm round cake
Oven temperature 350°F, 180°C

2 cups/250 g self-rising flour

¹/₂ cup/1 stick/125 g butter

¹/₂ cup/100 g superfine sugar

1 egg, beaten

1 tablespoon lemon juice

1 cup/200 g bottled fruit mincemeat

1 egg white, lightly beaten

extra superfine sugar

1 Sift flour into a large bowl. Cut in butter and stir in sugar, egg and lemon juice, mixing to form a firm dough. Cover and refrigerate for 30 minutes.

2 Divide dough in half. Roll one half large enough to cover bottom and sides of a greased 8 in/20 cm layer pan. Spread fruit mincemeat over dough.

3 Roll out remaining dough large enough to cover filling. Press edges together firmly. Brush lightly with egg white, sprinkle with extra sugar and bake for 30-35 minutes. Stand shortcake in pan for 10 minutes before turning onto a wire rack to cool.

COCONUT CAKE

Makes two 9 in/23 cm round layers
Oven temperature 350°F, 180°C

¹/₂ cup/1 stick/125 g butter or shortening, softened

1 teaspoon vanilla

1 cup/220 g superfine sugar

3 egg whites

2 cups/250 g self-rising flour, sifted

³/₄ cup/185 mL milk

1³/₄ cups/90 g dry shredded coconut

FLUFFY FROSTING

¹/₂ cup/125 mL water

1¹/₄ cups/315 g sugar

3 egg whites

1 teaspoon lemon juice

1 Place butter or shortening and vanilla in a bowl and beat until light and fluffy. Gradually add superfine sugar, beating well until mixture is creamy.

2 Beat in egg whites, one at a time. Fold flour and milk, alternately, into butter mixture. Divide batter evenly between two greased and floured lined 9 in/23 cm layer pans and bake for 25-30 minutes or until cakes are cooked when tested with a skewer. Stand in pans for 5 minutes before turning onto a wire rack to cool.

3 To make frosting, place water and sugar in a saucepan and cook over a medium heat, without boiling, stirring constantly until sugar dissolves. Brush any sugar from sides of pan using a pastry brush dipped in water. Bring syrup to the boil and boil rapidly for 3-5 minutes, without stirring, or until syrup reaches the soft-ball stage (239°F/115°C on a sugar thermometer). Place egg whites in a mixing bowl and beat until soft peaks form. Continue beating adding syrup slowly in a thin stream until all the syrup is used and frosting will stand in stiff peaks. Beat in lemon juice.

4 Spread one cake with a little frosting and sprinkle with 2 tablespoons coconut, then top with remaining cake. Spread remaining frosting over top and sides of cake and sprinkle with remaining coconut.

Cook's tip: This cake looks pretty when decorated with edible flowers such as violets, rose petals or borage.

ORANGE COCONUT LOAF

1 Place sugar, butter or shortening, vanilla and orange rind in a food processor and process until combined. Add coconut milk, egg whites, flour and baking powder and process until just combined and smooth.

2 Pour batter into a greased and floured lined 4¹⁄₂ x 8¹⁄₂ in/ 11 x 21 cm loaf pan and bake for 35-40 minutes or until cooked when tested with a skewer. Stand in pan for 5 minutes before turning onto a wire rack to cool.

Makes a 4¹⁄₂ x 8¹⁄₂ in/11 x 21 cm loaf
Oven temperature 350°F, 180°C

1 cup/220 g superfine sugar

¹⁄₃ cup/90 g butter or shortening, softened

1 teaspoon vanilla

1 tablespoon finely grated orange rind

³⁄₄ cup/185 mL coconut milk

3 egg whites

1²⁄₃ cups/200 g self-rising flour, sifted

1 teaspoon baking powder

OATY CHOC-CHIP COOKIES

1 Place butter or shortening, vanilla and sugar in a bowl and beat until light and creamy. Beat in egg, baking soda mixture and flour.

2 Stir in oats, coconut, chocolate chips and raisins. Place rounded tablespoons of mixture 4 in/10 cm apart on greased baking sheets. Using a knife, spread out each mound of mixture to form a thin 3 in/7.5 cm round. Bake for 8-10 minutes or until golden. Remove from oven and transfer to wire racks to cool.

Makes 25
Oven temperature 375°F, 190°C

¹⁄₂ cup/1 stick/125 g butter or shortening, softened

¹⁄₂ teaspoon vanilla

³⁄₄ cup/125 g packed brown sugar

1 egg

¹⁄₂ teaspoon baking soda dissolved in 4 teaspoons warm water

³⁄₄ cup/90 g flour, sifted

1¹⁄₂ cups/140 g rolled oats

¹⁄₂ cup/45 g grated dry coconut

6 oz/185 g semi-sweet chocolate chips

¹⁄₂ cup/75 g golden seedless raisins

GINGERSNAPS

Makes 45
Oven temperature 350°F, 180°C

1 cup/170 g packed brown sugar

1 tablespoon ground ginger

2 cups/250 g flour, sifted

¹/₂ cup/1 stick/125 g butter or shortening

1 cup/350 g light molasses

1 teaspoon baking soda

1   Place brown sugar, ginger and flour in a bowl and mix to combine.

2   Place butter or shortening and molasses in a saucepan and cook over a low heat, stirring, until butter or shortening melts. Stir in baking soda. Pour into dry ingredients and mix until smooth.

3   Drop teaspoons of mixture onto greased baking sheets and bake for 10-12 minutes or until golden. Remove from oven, loosen cookies with a spatula and allow to cool on sheets.

Cook's tip: As these cookies cool they become very crisp.

ORANGE POPPY SEED CAKE

1   Place poppy seeds, orange juice and yogurt in a bowl, mix to combine and set aside for 1 hour.

2   Place butter and orange rind in a large bowl and beat until light and fluffy. Gradually add sugar, beating well until mixture is light and creamy.

3   Add eggs one at a time, beating well after each addition. Fold flour and poppy seed mixture, alternately, into butter mixture.

4   Spoon batter into a greased and floured 8 in/20 cm fluted tube pan. Bake for 35-40 minutes or until cooked when tested with a skewer. Stand cake in pan for 5 minutes before turning onto a wire rack to cool.

Cook's tip: Recipe can be baked in a 6½-cup ring mold or 9 in/23 cm square baking pan, if desired.

Makes an 8 in/20 cm ring cake
Oven temperature 350°F, 180°C

$^1/_3$ **cup/90 mL poppy seeds**

$^1/_4$ **cup/60 mL orange juice**

$^1/_2$ **cup/125 g plain yogurt**

$^3/_4$ **cup/1$^1/_2$ sticks/185 g butter, softened**

1 tablespoon finely grated orange rind

1 cup/220 g superfine sugar

3 eggs

2 cups/250 g self-rising flour, sifted

Left: Shortbread Creams (page 42), Afghan Cookies (page 42), Gingersnaps
Above: Orange Poppy Seed Cake, Yogurt Pound Cake (page 43)

AFGHAN COOKIES

Makes 30
Oven temperature 400°F, 200°C

3/4 cup/1¹/₂ sticks/185 g butter or shortening, softened

1 teaspoon vanilla

¹/₂ cup/100 g superfine sugar

1¹/₂ cups/185 g flour

1 teaspoon baking powder

4 teaspoons cocoa powder

2 cups/90 g corn flakes, crushed

3 tablespoons golden seedless raisins, chopped

slivered almonds

CHOCOLATE FROSTING

1 tablespoon/15 g butter, softened

4 teaspoons cocoa powder

1 cup/155 g confectioners' sugar, sifted

1 tablespoon water

1   Place butter or shortening and vanilla in a mixing bowl and beat until light and fluffy. Gradually add sugar, beating well until mixture is creamy.

2   Sift together flour, baking powder and cocoa powder. Stir into butter mixture, then fold in corn flakes and raisins. Place heaped teaspoons of mixture on greased baking sheets and bake for 12-15 minutes. Transfer to wire racks to cool.

3   To make frosting, combine butter and cocoa powder with confectioners' sugar in a small bowl and mix in water until frosting is of an easy-to-spread consistency.

4   Place a teaspoon of frosting on each cookie and sprinkle with almonds. Set aside until frosting firms.

SHORTBREAD CREAMS

Makes 24
Oven temperature 350°F, 180°C

1 cup/2 sticks/250 g butter, softened

¹/₃ cup/50g confectioners' sugar, sifted

1 cup/125 g cornstarch

1 cup/125 g flour

LEMON FILLING

¹/₄ cup/¹/₂ stick/60 g butter, softened

¹/₂ cup/75 g confectioners' sugar

2 teaspoons finely grated lemon rind

1 tablespoon lemon juice

1   Place butter and confectioners' sugar in a large bowl and beat until light and fluffy. Sift cornstarch and flour together and stir into butter mixture.

2   Spoon mixture into a large pastry bag fitted with a large star tube and pipe small rosettes on greased baking sheets, leaving space between each rosette. Bake for 15-20 minutes or until a pale golden color. Cool cookies on sheets.

3   To make filling, place butter in a bowl and beat until light and fluffy. Gradually add confectioners' sugar and beat until creamy. Stir in lemon rind and lemon juice. Using filling, sandwich each two cookies together.

YOGURT POUND CAKE

Makes a 9 in/23 cm square cake
Oven temperature 325°F, 160°C

1 cup/2 sticks/250 g butter or shortening, softened

2 teaspoons vanilla

1 teaspoon finely grated lemon rind

2 cups/440 g superfine sugar

6 eggs

1¹/₂ cups/185 g flour

1 cup/125 g self-rising flour

8 oz/250 g plain yogurt

LEMON FROSTING

1¹/₂ cups/220 g confectioners' sugar, sifted

1 tablespoon lemon juice

2 tablespoons/30 g butter, softened

2 tablespoons dry shredded coconut, toasted

1   Place butter or shortening, vanilla and lemon rind in a large mixing bowl and beat until light and fluffy. Gradually add sugar, beating well until mixture is creamy.

2   Add eggs one at a time, beating well after each addition. Sift flour and self-rising flour together. Fold flour mixture and yogurt, alternately, into butter or shortening mixture. Spoon batter into a 3 in/7.5 cm deep, greased and lined 9 in/23 cm square cake pan. Bake for 1 hour or until cake is cooked when tested with a skewer. Stand in pan for 10 minutes before turning onto a wire rack to cool.

3   To make frosting, place confectioners' sugar, lemon juice and butter in a bowl and mix until smooth. Add a little more lemon juice if necessary. Spread frosting over cold cake and sprinkle with coconut.

Cook's tip: Recipe can be baked in a greased and floured 8 in/20 cm fluted tube pan, if desired.

LIME AND COCONUT COOKIES

Makes 35
Oven temperature 350°F, 180°C

¹/₂ cup/1 stick/125 g butter or shortening, chopped

1 cup/170 g packed brown sugar

1 teaspoon vanilla

1 egg

1 cup/125 g flour

¹/₂ cup/60 g self-rising flour

1 cup/90 g rolled oats

¹/₂ cup/45 g grated dry coconut

2 teaspoons finely grated lime rind

2-3 tablespoons lime juice

1   Place butter or shortening, sugar, vanilla, egg, flour, self-rising flour, rolled oats, coconut, lime rind and lime juice in a food processor and process until well combined.

2   Place heaped spoonfuls of mixture on greased baking sheets and bake for 12-15 minutes or until lightly browned. Remove from oven and transfer to wire racks to cool.

No Fussin' Muffins

Makes 12
Oven temperature 350°F, 180°C

1³/₄ cups/280 g wholewheat flour,
sifted and grits returned

2¹/₂ teaspoons baking powder

³/₄ teaspoon salt

¹/₂ cup/90 g packed brown sugar

1 egg, lightly beaten

³/₄ cup/185 mL milk

¹/₄ cup/¹/₂ stick/60 g butter, melted

1   Combine flour, baking powder, salt and sugar in a large bowl. Stir in egg, milk and butter and mix well.

2   Spoon mixture into 12 lightly greased muffin cups and bake for 20-25 minutes, or until cooked and golden brown.

Carrot and Walnut Muffins: Stir 5 oz/155 g shredded carrot, ¹/₄ cup/30 g chopped walnuts and ¹/₂ teaspoon ground cinnamon into the basic mixture.

Almond and Ginger Muffins: Stir ¹/₄ cup/30 g ground almonds, 2 tablespoons finely chopped crystallized ginger and 2 teaspoons grated orange rind into the basic mixture.

Cranberry Muffins: Stir ¹/₂ cup/170 g cranberry sauce into the basic mixture .

Banana and Pecan Muffins: Stir 3 mashed ripe bananas and ¹/₄ cup/30 g chopped pecans into the basic mixture. Combine ¹/₄ cup/45 g packed brown sugar, ¹/₄ cup/30 g finely chopped pecans and 1 teaspoon ground cinnamon, and sprinkle over muffins before cooking.

GINGER 'N' FRUIT COOKIES

1   Place flour, baking powder, sugar, fruit and ginger in a large bowl and mix.

2   Gradually stir in oil, egg whites and milk. Mix well.

3   Place spoonfuls of mixture on a lightly greased baking sheet and top with a cherry half. Bake for 12-15 minutes or until golden. Remove from oven and transfer to wire racks to cool.

Makes 18
Oven temperature 350°F, 180°C

1½ cups/230 g wholewheat flour, sifted and grits returned

2 teaspoons baking powder

¼ cup/45 g packed brown sugar

¼ cup/45 g diced mixed dried and candied fruits and peels

1 tablespoon chopped crystallized ginger

2 tablespoons olive oil

3 egg whites, lightly beaten

⅓ cup/90 mL milk

9 candied cherries, halved

Ginger 'n' Fruit Cookies and a variety of No Fussin' Muffins

LADYFINGERS

Makes 20
Oven temperature 375°F, 190°C

2 eggs
³/₄ cup/170 g superfine sugar
1 cup/125 g flour

1   Place eggs and ¹/₂ cup/100 g of the sugar in a bowl and beat for 8-10 minutes or until mixture is thick and creamy and leaves a trail when the beaters are lifted from the mixture.

2   Sift flour three times, then fold into egg mixture. Spoon batter into a pastry bag fitted with ³/₄ in/2 cm plain tube and pipe 3 in/8 cm lengths onto greased and lined baking sheets. Sprinkle with remaining sugar and bake for 5-7 minutes or until lightly colored and cooked. Allow cookies to cool on sheets.

Cook's tip: These lovely little cake-like cookies can be eaten as they are or used as a base for cheesecakes and refrigerated desserts.

CARROT AND ALMOND CAKE

Makes a 7 x 11 in/18 x 28 cm cake
Oven temperature 350°F, 180°C

1 cup/155 g wholewheat flour
¹/₄ cup/30 g wheat germ
1¹/₄ teaspoons baking soda
1 teaspoon ground cinnamon
1 teaspoon ground nutmeg
¹/₂ teaspoon cream of tartar
¹/₂ cup/125 mL vegetable oil
²/₃ cup/230 g honey
3 eggs, lightly beaten
1 carrot, shredded
¹/₂ cup/60 g chopped walnuts
4 oz/125 g well-drained canned crushed pineapple
¹/₃ cup/60 g candied cherries, halved
¹/₃ cup/60 g blanched almonds

1   Sift flour, wheat germ, baking soda, cinnamon and nutmeg and cream of tartar together into a bowl. Return grits to bowl. Place oil, honey and eggs in a separate bowl and beat until well combined. Pour oil mixture into flour mixture and beat for 1 minute or until mixture is smooth.

2   Stir in carrot, walnuts and pineapple. Spoon batter into a shallow, greased and lined 7 x 11 in/18 x 28 cm cake pan and decorate top with cherries and almonds. Bake for 35-40 minutes or until cake is cooked when tested with a skewer. Stand in pan for 5 minutes before turning onto a wire rack to cool.

APPLE SLICE CAKE

1 To make topping, melt butter in a skillet. Add apples and cook over a medium heat for 3-5 minutes or until tender. Remove pan from heat and set aside.

2 Place butter or shortening and vanilla in a bowl and beat until light and fluffy. Gradually add sugar, beating well until mixture is light and creamy.

3 Add eggs one at a time, beating well after each addition. Sift together flour and baking powder. Fold flour mixture and milk, alternately, into butter mixture. Spoon batter into a 3 in/7.5 cm deep, greased and lined 8 in/20 cm round cake pan or springform.

4 Arrange apple mixture on top of cake. Combine sugar and cinnamon and sprinkle over top of cake. Bake for 40-45 minutes or until cooked when tested with a skewer. Stand in pan for 5 minutes before turning onto a wire rack to cool.

Makes a deep 8 in/20 cm round cake
Oven temperature 350°F, 180°C

¹/₂ cup/1 stick/125 g butter or shortening, softened

1 teaspoon vanilla

²/₃ cup/140 g superfine sugar

2 eggs

2 cups/250 g flour

1 tablespoon baking powder

¹/₂ cup/125 mL milk

APPLE TOPPING

2 tablespoons/30 g butter

1 green apple, cored, peeled and thinly sliced

1 tablespoon superfine sugar

2 teaspoons cinnamon

APPLE AND BLUEBERRY CAKE

1 Place butter, vanilla, sugar, eggs, flour and milk in a bowl and beat well until ingredients are combined and mixture is smooth.

2 Spoon half the batter into a 3 in/7.5 cm deep, greased and lined 8 in/20 cm round cake pan or springform pan. Top with half the apple slices and half the blueberries, then remaining batter. Arrange remaining apple and blueberries over top of batter.

3 To make topping, combine sugar and cinnamon and sprinkle over cake. Bake for 55-60 minutes or until cake is cooked when tested with a skewer. Stand in pan for 10 minutes before turning onto a wire rack to cool.

Variation: You may like to try replacing the blueberries in this recipe with canned blackberries.

Cook's tip: To make soured milk, stir 2 teaspoons cider vinegar into ¹/₂ cup milk and let stand until curdled, about 10 minutes.

Makes a deep 8 in/20 cm round cake
Oven temperature 350°F, 180°C

¹/₂ cup/1 stick/125 g butter, softened

1 teaspoon vanilla

³/₄ cup/170 g superfine sugar

2 eggs, lightly beaten

1¹/₂ cups/185 g self-rising flour, sifted

¹/₂ cup/125 mL buttermilk or soured milk

7 oz/220 g canned apple slices, drained

7 oz/220 g canned blueberries, well drained

CINNAMON TOPPING

1 tablespoon superfine sugar

1 teaspoon ground cinnamon

HAZELNUT SHORTBREAD

Makes 40
Oven temperature 325°F, 160°C

1½ cups/185 g flour, sifted

1½ oz/45 g hazelnuts (filberts), ground

¼ cup/45 g ground rice (rice flour)

1 cup/2 sticks/250 g butter, cut into small pieces

¼ cup/60 g superfine sugar

4 oz/125 g semi-sweet cooking chocolate, melted

1   Place flour, hazelnuts (filberts), ground rice (rice flour) and butter in a food processor and process until mixture resembles coarse bread crumbs. Add sugar and process to combine.

2   Turn mixture onto a lightly floured surface and knead to make a pliable dough. Place dough between sheets of parchment paper and roll out to ¼ in/5 mm thick. Using a 2 in/5 cm fluted cutter, cut out rounds of dough and place 1 in/2.5 cm apart on greased baking sheets. Bake for 20-25 minutes or until lightly browned. Stand on sheets for 2-3 minutes before transferring to wire racks to cool.

3   Place melted chocolate in a plastic bag, snip off one corner and pipe lines across each cookie.

WALNUT HONEY BAKLAVA

Makes 20
Oven temperature 425°F, 220°C

12 oz/375 g fillo (phyllo) pastry

½ cup/1 stick/125 g plus 2 tablespoons/30 g butter, melted

WALNUT FILLING
2 cups/250 g finely chopped walnuts, toasted

1 teaspoon ground cinnamon

1 teaspoon pumpkin pie spice

⅓ cup/60 g packed brown sugar

HONEY ORANGE SYRUP
½ cup/125 mL water

⅓ cup/90 g sugar

⅓ cup/125 g honey

⅓ cup/90 mL orange juice

3 tablespoons lemon juice

1   To make filling, place walnuts, cinnamon, pie spice and brown sugar in a bowl. Mix to combine and set aside.

2   Cut pastry sheets into 7 x 11 in/18 x 28 cm rectangles. Layer a quarter of the pastry sheets in a shallow, greased 7 x 11 in/18 x 28 cm cake pan, brushing each sheet with butter. Sprinkle pastry with one-third of the filling, repeat with remaining pastry and filling, finishing with a layer of pastry.

3   Cut pastry into squares using a sharp knife. Brush top with butter and bake for 15 minutes. Reduce oven temperature to 375°F/190°C and bake for 10 minutes longer or until golden brown.

4   To make syrup, place water, sugar, honey, orange juice and lemon juice in a small saucepan and cook over a medium heat, stirring constantly, until sugar dissolves. Bring to the boil, then remove from heat and pour over hot baklava. Set aside and allow to cool in pan.

Apple and Blueberry Cake (page 47), Walnut Honey Baklava, Hazelnut Shortbread

LEMON AND LIME BARS

Makes 30
Oven temperature 375°F, 190°C

¹/₂ cup/1 stick/125 g butter or shortening

1 cup/125 g flour

¹/₂ cup/75 g confectioners' sugar

confectioners' sugar, to dust

LEMON AND LIME TOPPING
2 eggs, lightly beaten

1 cup/220 g superfine sugar

4 teaspoons flour

4 teaspoons lemon juice

3 tablespoons lime juice

1 teaspoon finely grated lemon rind

1   Place butter or shortening, flour and confectioners' sugar in a food processor and process to form a soft dough. Turn dough onto a lightly floured surface and knead briefly. Press dough into a shallow, greased and lined 7 x 11 in/18 x 28 cm cake pan and bake for 20 minutes or until firm. Allow to cool in pan.

2   To make topping, place eggs, sugar, flour, lemon juice, lime juice and lemon rind in a bowl and mix until combined. Pour topping over cooked layer and cook for 25-30 minutes or until firm. Refrigerate until cold, then cut into bars. Just prior to serving, dust with confectioners' sugar.

Below: Easy Lemon and Almond Cake (page 52), Lemon and Lime Bars
Right: Choc-Chip and Orange Cake (page 52),
Lemon Marshmallow Squares (page 53), Orange Pecan Loaf (page 53)

EASY LEMON AND ALMOND CAKE

Makes a deep 8 in/20 cm round cake
Oven temperature 350°F, 180°C

³/₄ cup/1¹/₂ sticks/185 g butter or shortening, softened

¹/₂ cup/100 g superfine sugar

¹/₂ cup/185 g prepared lemon curd

3 eggs, lightly beaten

1¹/₄ cups/155 g self-rising flour, sifted

¹/₄ cup/30 g ground almonds

¹/₂ cup/125 mL milk

¹/₄ cup/30 g sliced almonds, toasted

LEMON FROSTING

4 oz/125 g cream cheese

1 teaspoon finely grated lemon rind

1¹/₂ cups/230 g confectioners' sugar

2 teaspoons lemon juice

1   Place butter or shortening, sugar, lemon curd, eggs, flour, ground almonds and milk in a large bowl and beat well.

2   Spoon batter into a 3 in/7.5 cm deep, greased and lined 8 in/20 cm round cake pan or springform pan and bake for 40 minutes or until cooked when tested with a skewer. Stand cake in pan for 5 minutes before turning onto a wire rack to cool.

3   To make frosting, place cream cheese, lemon rind, confectioners' sugar and lemon juice in a food processor and process for 1 minute or until frosting is of an easy-to-spread consistency. Spread frosting over top of cold cake. Sprinkle with sliced almonds.

Cook's tip: If self-rising flour is unavailable, substitute with 1¹/₄ cups/220 g all-purpose flour sifted with ¹/₂ teaspoon cream of tartar and ¹/₄ teaspoon baking powder.

CHOC-CHIP AND ORANGE CAKE

Makes an 8 in/20 cm ring cake
Oven temperature 350°F, 180°C

¹/₂ cup/1 stick/125 g butter or shortening, softened

2 teaspoons grated orange rind

³/₄ cup/170 g superfine sugar

2 eggs, lightly beaten

1¹/₂ cups/185 g self-rising flour, sifted

2 tablespoons orange juice

¹/₂ cup/100 g plain yogurt

¹/₄ cup/60 mL milk

4 oz/125 g semi-sweet cooking chocolate, coarsely grated

CHOCOLATE GLAZE

3 tablespoons/45 g butter, softened

¹/₂ teaspoon grated orange rind

³/₄ cup/125 g confectioners' sugar, sifted

1¹/₂ tablespoons cocoa powder, sifted

1 tablespoon orange juice

1   Place butter or shortening , orange rind, sugar, eggs, flour, orange juice, yogurt and milk in a large bowl and beat until ingredients are combined and batter is smooth. Fold in grated chocolate.

2   Spoon batter into a greased 8 in/20 cm fluted tube pan and bake for 45-50 minutes or until cake is cooked when tested with a skewer. Stand cake in pan for 5 minutes before turning onto a wire rack to cool.

3   To make glaze, place butter and orange rind in a mixing bowl and beat until creamy. Add confectioners' sugar, cocoa powder and orange juice and beat until combined. Add a little more orange juice if necessary. Place in top of a double boiler set over simmering water and cook, stirring constantly, for 2-3 minutes or until mixture is smooth and runny. Pour glaze over cold cake.

Cook's tip: Recipe can be baked in a 6¹/₂-cup ring mold or 2 in/5 cm deep, 9 in/23 cm square baking pan, if desired.

1 Sift together flour, self-rising flour, baking soda, cardamom and nutmeg into a large bowl.

2 Place eggs and sugar in a bowl and beat until light and creamy. Gradually add oil, beating well until mixture is thick and increased in volume. Mix in vanilla, orange juice and orange rind. Fold flour mixture into egg mixture, then mix in carrots and pecans.

3 Spoon mixture into a greased and floured 4½ x 8½ in/11 x 21 cm loaf pan and bake for 50 minutes or until cooked when tested with a skewer. Stand in pan for 5 minutes before turning onto a wire rack to cool.

ORANGE PECAN LOAF

Makes a 4½ x 8½ in/11 x 21 cm loaf
Oven temperature 350°F, 180°C

½ cup/60 g flour

1 cup/125 g self-rising flour

½ teaspoon baking soda

½ teaspoon ground cardamom

½ teaspoon ground nutmeg

2 eggs

1 cup/220 g superfine sugar

½ cup/125 mL vegetable oil

½ teaspoon vanilla

1 tablespoon orange juice

2 teaspoons finely grated orange rind

100 g/3½ oz carrots, shredded

⅔ cup/60 g pecans, chopped

LEMON MARSHMALLOW SQUARES

1 Place wafer crumbs, butter and coconut in a bowl and mix well to combine. Press mixture into a shallow, greased and lined 7 x 11 in/18 x 28 cm cake pan. Refrigerate until firm.

2 To make filling, place marshmallows, gelatin, milk, lemon juice and lemon rind in a saucepan. Cook over a low heat, stirring, until mixture is smooth and gelatin dissolves. Remove pan from heat and set aside to cool, stirring every 3-5 minutes. Pour filling over cookie layer and refrigerate until firm. Cut into squares.

Lime Marshmallow Squares: Replace lemon juice and lemon rind with lime juice and lime rind.

Makes 30

1 cup/100 g vanilla wafer crumbs

¼ cup/½ stick/60 g butter, melted

⅓ cup/30 g grated dry coconut

LEMON MARSHMALLOW
TOPPING
12½ oz/400 g white marshmallows

4 teaspoons unflavored gelatin

⅔ cup/170 mL milk

⅓ cup/90 mL lemon juice

½ cup/90 g finely grated lemon rind

CRUNCHY ALMOND HONEY BARS

Makes 30

1 tablespoon/15 g butter

½ cup/170 g honey

2 oz/60 g sliced almonds, toasted

⅓ cup/90 mL sunflower seeds

3 tablespoons sesame seeds

⅔ cup/60 g grated dry coconut

1 cup/30 g crisp rice cereal

LEMON GLAZE

1½ cups/230 g confectioners' sugar, sifted

1 tablespoon/15 g butter

2 tablespoons lemon juice

1 tablespoon water

From right: Chocolate Potato Cake (page 56), Chocolate Caramel Squares, Honey Banana Cake (page 56), Crunchy Almond Honey Bars

1 Place butter and honey in a saucepan and bring to the boil, stirring. Add almonds, sunflower and sesame seeds and boil gently, without stirring, for 3 minutes.

2 Remove pan from heat. Stir in coconut and rice cereal. Spread into a shallow 7 x 11 in/18 x 28 cm cake pan lined with aluminum foil and press down firmly. Refrigerate until set.

3 To make glaze, place confectioners' sugar, butter, lemon juice and water in a mixing bowl and beat until smooth.

4 Remove layer from pan. Spread with glaze. Cut into bars.

CHOCOLATE CARAMEL SQUARES

1 To make base, place butter and sugar in a bowl and beat until light and fluffy. Mix in cornstarch and flour. Turn onto a lightly floured surface and knead briefly, then press into a shallow, greased and lined 7 x 11 in/18 x 28 cm cake pan. Bake for 25 minutes or until firm.

2 To make filling, place butter, brown sugar and honey in a saucepan and heat, stirring until sugar dissolves. Bring to the boil and simmer for 7 minutes, then add condensed milk and vanilla and beat well. Pour filling over baked layer and bake for 20 minutes. Allow to cool completely.

3 Spread melted chocolate over filling and set aside until firm. Cut into squares.

Makes 25
Oven temperature 350°F, 180°C

6 oz/185 g semi-sweet cooking chocolate, melted

SHORTBREAD BASE
$^{1}/_{3}$ cup/90 g butter

$^{1}/_{4}$ cup/60 g sugar

$^{1}/_{2}$ cup/60 g cornstarch, sifted

1 cup/125 g flour, sifted

CARAMEL FILLING
$^{1}/_{2}$ cup/1 stick/125 g butter

$^{1}/_{2}$ cup/90 g packed brown sugar

2 tablespoons honey

12$^{1}/_{2}$ oz/400 g sweetened condensed milk

1 teaspoon vanilla

GINGER COOKIES

Makes 48
Oven temperature 350°F, 180°C

³/₄ cup/1¹/₂ sticks/185 g butter or shortening

³/₄ cup/185 g sugar

2 cups/250 g flour

pinch salt

¹/₄ cup/45 g almonds, chopped

3 tablespoons/45 g preserved ginger in syrup, coarsely chopped

1 egg

1 egg yolk beaten with 1 tablespoon water

1   Place butter or shortening in a food processor and process until light and creamy. Add sugar, flour, salt, almonds, ginger and egg and process to make a stiff dough.

2   Turn dough onto a lightly floured surface. Knead briefly then roll into 1 in/2.5 cm thick logs. Wrap logs in aluminum foil and refrigerate for 30 minutes or until firm.

3   Cut logs into ¹/₄ in/5 mm slices and place on lightly greased baking sheets. Brush with egg yolk mixture and bake for 15 minutes. Stand cookies on sheets for 3-5 minutes before transferring to wire racks to cool.

CHRISTMAS COOKIES

Makes 25
Oven temperature 350°F, 180°C

¹/₂ cup/1 stick/125 g butter or shortening

1 cup/220 g superfine sugar

1 egg, lightly beaten

2 teaspoons vanilla

¹/₄ cup/60 mL milk

1¹/₄ cups/155 g flour

¹/₂ teaspoon baking soda

3 oz/90 g roasted hazelnuts (filberts), chopped

4 oz/125 g semi-sweet chocolate chips

1³/₄ cups/90 g shredded dry coconut

¹/₂ cup/90 g golden seedless raisins

¹/₂ cup/90 g candied cherries, chopped

1   Place butter or shortening and sugar in a bowl and beat until light and fluffy. Beat in egg, vanilla and milk.

2   Sift together flour and baking soda and stir into butter mixture. Add hazelnuts (filberts), chocolate chips, coconut, raisins and cherries and mix well.

3   Drop tablespoons of mixture onto greased baking sheets and bake for 15 minutes or until golden. Remove from oven and transfer to wire racks to cool.

HONEY BANANA CAKE

Makes a deep 9 in/23 cm square cake
Oven temperature 325°F, 160°C

1 cup/155 g wholewheat flour

1 cup/125 g self-rising flour

1¹/₄ teaspoons baking soda

1 teaspoon ground nutmeg

¹/₂ teaspoon cream of tartar

³/₄ cup/185 g granulated brown (raw or demerara) sugar

2 tablespoons honey, warmed

4 eggs, lightly beaten

5 ripe bananas, mashed

1 cup/250 mL vegetable oil

HONEY CHEESE TOPPING
4 oz/125 g cream cheese

2 tablespoons honey

ground nutmeg

1   Sift wholewheat flour, self-rising flour, baking soda, nutmeg and cream of tartar together into a large bowl. Return grits to bowl. Stir in sugar, honey, eggs, bananas and oil and beat until smooth.

2   Pour batter into a 3 in/7.5 cm deep, greased and lined 9 in/23 cm square cake pan. Bake for 1 hour or until cooked when tested with a skewer. Stand cake in pan for 10 minutes before turning onto a wire rack to cool.

3   To make topping, place cream cheese and honey in a bowl and beat until smooth and creamy. Spread topping over cold cake and sprinkle with nutmeg.

Cook's tip: Recipe can be baked in a greased and floured 1¹/₂ x 7 x 11 in/4 x 18 x 28 cm cake pan, if desired.

CHOCOLATE POTATO CAKE

Makes a deep 9 in/23 cm round cake
Oven temperature 350°F, 180°C

¹/₂ cup/1 stick/125 g butter or shortening

155 g/5 oz superfine sugar

1 large potato, cooked and mashed

2 oz/60 g semi-sweet cooking chocolate, melted

¹/₄ cup/30 g cocoa powder, sifted

2 eggs

1 tablespoon lemon juice

1¹/₂ cups/185 g self-rising flour, sifted with ¹/₂ teaspoon ground nutmeg

²/₃ cup/60 g walnuts, chopped

¹/₄ cup/60 mL milk

SOUR CREAM CHOCOLATE FROSTING
5 oz/155 g semi-sweet cooking chocolate, melted

1 cup/250 g dairy sour cream

1   Place butter or shortening in a large bowl and beat until light and creamy. Add sugar a little at a time, beating well after each addition. Beat in potato, chocolate and cocoa powder. Then beat in eggs, one at a time. Stir in lemon juice.

2   Combine flour mixture and walnuts. Fold flour mixture and milk, alternately, into chocolate mixture. Spoon batter into a 3 in/7.5 cm deep, greased and lined 9 in/23 cm round cake pan or springform pan and bake for 35-40 minutes, or until cooked when tested with a skewer. Stand in pan for 5 minutes before turning onto a wire rack to cool.

3   To make frosting, place chocolate and sour cream in a mixing bowl and beat until combined. Spread frosting over cold cake.

JELLY ROLL

Serves 8-10
Oven temperature 375°F, 190°C

4 eggs

¹/₂ cup/100 g superfine sugar

1 cup/125 g self-rising flour

¹/₃ cup/90 mL hot milk

¹/₂ cup/125 mL whipping cream, whipped (optional)

4 oz/125 g strawberries, sliced, or 2 tablespoons raspberry jam

confectioners' sugar, sifted

Below: Christmas Cookies (page 57)
Right: Jelly Roll

1　Place eggs and sugar in a bowl and beat until thick and creamy. This will take about 8-10 minutes.

2　Sift flour three times and fold in egg mixture. Fold milk into batter and pour into a greased and lined 10¹/₂ x 12³/₄ in/ 26 x 32 cm jelly roll pan and bake for 20-25 minutes or until cake springs back when touched with the fingertips.

3　Turn cake onto a damp teatowel sprinkled with superfine sugar. Carefully remove lining paper from cake and roll up from short end. Set aside to cool.

4　Unroll cake, spread with whipped cream and strawberries. Reroll, sprinkle with confectioners' sugar and serve. Alternatively, the cake can be spread with raspberry jam and cream or just with raspberry jam.

Cook's tip: When making a sponge cake you need to beat the egg mixture until it is very thick and creamy. This will take 8-10 minutes using an electric mixer. At the completion of beating, a thick ribbon trail will be left when the beaters are lifted from the mixture.

COFFEE OAT AND DATE BARS

Makes a deep 9 in/23 cm square cake
Oven temperature 350°F, 180°C

¹/₂ cup/1 stick/125 g butter or shortening, softened

4 teaspoons instant coffee powder dissolved in 4 teaspoons hot water, cooled

³/₄ cup/170 g superfine sugar

2 eggs, lightly beaten

1¹/₂ cups/185 g self-rising flour, sifted

¹/₂ cup/125 mL buttermilk or soured milk

DATE AND OAT TOPPING
6¹/₂ oz/200 g pitted dates, chopped

²/₃ cup/170 mL water

2 tablespoons superfine sugar

¹/₄ cup/30 g rolled oats

1 tablespoon packed brown sugar

2 tablespoons self-rising flour

2 tablespoons/30 g butter, melted

1 tablespoon chopped walnuts

1　To make topping, place dates, water and superfine sugar in a saucepan and cook over a medium heat, stirring, for 3-4 minutes or until dates are soft and mixture thickens slightly. Remove pan from heat and set aside to cool. Place oats, brown sugar and flour in a bowl, stir in butter and walnuts and set aside.

2　Place butter, coffee mixture, superfine sugar, eggs, flour and buttermilk or soured milk in a large bowl and beat until mixture is smooth. Spoon batter into a 3 in/7.5 cm deep, greased and lined 9 in/23 cm square cake pan, top with date mixture and sprinkle over oat mixture. Bake for 40-45 minutes or until cooked when tested with a skewer. Stand in pan for 10 minutes before turning onto a wire rack to cool.

Cook's tips: Recipe can be baked in a greased and lined 1¹/₂ x 7 x 11 in/4 x 18 x 28 cm cake pan, if desired.

To make soured milk, stir 2 teaspoons cider vinegar into ¹/₂ cup milk and let stand until curdled, about 10 minutes.

MOCHA FUDGE

Makes 30 squares

1 lb/500 g semi-sweet cooking chocolate

1 cup/250 mL sweetened condensed milk

2 tablespoons/30 g butter

1 tablespoon instant coffee powder

Place chocolate, condensed milk, butter and coffee powder in a small saucepan and cook over a low heat, stirring, until mixture is smooth. Pour fudge into a 8 in/20 cm square cake pan lined with aluminum foil and refrigerate for 2 hours or until set. Cut into squares.

COFFEE CUPCAKES

Makes 12
Oven temperature 400°F, 200°C

1 Place flour, sugar, eggs, coffee mixture, butter and milk in a large bowl and beat until ingredients are well combined and mixture is smooth.

2 Spoon batter into muffin cups lined with paper bake cups and bake for 15-18 minutes or until cakes are well risen and cooked when tested with a skewer. Remove cakes from cups and cool on a wire rack.

3 To make frosting, place confectioners' sugar, butter and coffee mixture in a bowl and beat to make a frosting with an easy-to-spread consistency. Spread frosting over cold cakes and top with chocolate sprinkles or coffee beans.

1¹/₂ cups/185 g self-rising flour, sifted

¹/₂ cup/100 g superfine sugar

2 eggs, lightly beaten

2 teaspoons instant coffee powder dissolved in 2 teaspoons hot water, cooled

¹/₄ cup/¹/₂ stick/60 g butter, melted

¹/₂ cup/125 mL milk

COFFEE FROSTING
1¹/₂ cups/220 g confectioners' sugar, sifted

2 teaspoons butter, softened

1 teaspoon instant coffee powder dissolved in 1¹/₂ teaspoons hot water, cooled

chocolate sprinkles or candy coffee beans

GOLDEN OAT COOKIES

Makes 30
Oven temperature 350°F, 180°C

1 Place oats, flour, coconut and sugar in a large mixing bowl. Combine honey or molasses, butter, water and baking soda.

2 Pour syrup mixture into dry ingredients and mix well. Place spoonfuls of mixture 1¹/₄ in/3 cm apart on greased baking sheets and bake for 10-15 minutes or until cookies are just firm. Stand on sheets for 3 minutes before transferring to wire racks to cool.

1 cup/90 g rolled oats

1 cup/125 g flour, sifted

1 cup/90 g grated dry coconut

1 cup/250 g sugar

4 teaspoons honey or light molasses, warmed

¹/₂ cup/1 stick/125 g butter, melted

2 tablespoons boiling water

1 teaspoon baking soda

COFFEE LAYER CAKE

Makes two 7 in/18 cm round layers
Oven temperature 325°F, 160°C

1 cup/2 sticks/250 g butter or shortening, softened

1 cup/220 g superfine sugar

6 eggs, lightly beaten

2 cups/250 g self-rising flour, sifted

4 teaspoons baking powder

COFFEE FROSTING

¼ cup/½ stick/60 g butter, softened

¾ cup/125 g confectioners' sugar, sifted

½ teaspoon ground cinnamon

2 teaspoons instant coffee powder dissolved in 2 teaspoons hot water, cooled

LIQUEUR CREAM FILLING

1 tablespoon coffee-flavored liqueur

½ cup/125 mL whipping cream, whipped

1   Place butter or shortening and sugar in a food processor and process until creamy. Add eggs, flour and baking powder and process until all ingredients are combined. Spoon batter into two greased and lined 7 in/18 cm round cake pans and bake for 30-35 minutes or until golden. Turn onto wire racks to cool.

2   To make frosting, place butter, confectioners' sugar, cinnamon and coffee mixture in a food processor and process until fluffy.

3   To make filling, fold liqueur into whipped cream. Spread filling over one cake and top with remaining cake. Spread frosting over top of cake.

Cook's tip: For a nonalcoholic version dissolve 1 teaspoon instant coffee powder in 1 teaspoon hot water, cool, then fold into whipped cream. This cake can be baked as one layer in a 3 in/7.5 cm deep, greased and lined 8 or 9 in/20 or 23 cm springform pan, if desired. When cool, split layer in half horizontally to fill and frost.

Below: Coffee Layer Cake, Right: Coffee Cupcakes (page 61), Coffee Oat and Date Bars (page 60), Mocha Fudge (page 60)

COFFEE KISSES

Makes 25
Oven temperature 350°F, 180°C

1 cup/2 sticks/250 g butter, softened

²/₃ cup/100 g confectioners' sugar, sifted

2 teaspoons instant coffee powder dissolved in 1 tablespoon hot water, cooled

2 cups/250 g flour, sifted

2 oz/60 g semi-sweet cooking chocolate, melted

confectioners' sugar

1   Place butter and confectioners' sugar in a large bowl and beat until light and fluffy. Stir in coffee mixture and flour.

2   Spoon dough into a pastry bag fitted with a medium star tube and pipe ³/₄ in/2 cm rounds of mixture ³/₄ in/2 cm apart on greased baking sheets. Bake for 10-12 minutes or until lightly browned. Stand on sheets for 5 minutes before transferring to wire racks to cool.

3   Join cookies with a little melted chocolate, then dust with confectioners' sugar.

CRUNCHY CARAMEL CAKE

Makes a deep 9 in/23 cm square cake
Oven temperature 350°F, 180°C

¹/₂ cup/1 stick/125 g butter or shortening, softened

3 tablespoons honey or light molasses

¹/₂ cup/90 g packed brown sugar

2 eggs, lightly beaten

1¹/₂ cups/185 g self-rising flour, sifted

¹/₂ cup/125 mL milk

CRUNCHY TOPPING
³/₄ cup/75 g rolled oats

¹/₄ cup/30 g flour

2 tablespoons/15 g grated dry coconut

2 tablespoons packed brown sugar

3 tablespoons/45 g butter, melted

CARAMEL FROSTING
¹/₄ cup/¹/₂ stick/60 g butter

1¹/₂ cups/220 g confectioners' sugar

1¹/₂ tablespoons honey or light molasses

1   Place butter or shortening, honey or molasses, sugar, eggs, flour and milk in a large bowl. Beat well until ingredients are combined and batter is smooth.

2   Spoon batter into a 3 in/7.5 cm deep, greased and lined 9 in/23 cm square cake pan and bake for 40-45 minutes or until cake is cooked when tested with a skewer. Stand in pan for 10 minutes before turning onto a wire rack to cool.

3   To make topping, place rolled oats, flour, coconut and sugar in a bowl and mix to combine. Stir in butter, then spread mixture on a greased baking sheet and bake for 10 minutes or until golden and crunchy.

4   To make frosting, place butter in a small bowl and beat until light and creamy. Add confectioners' sugar and honey or molasses and beat until smooth. Spread frosting over cold cake then sprinkle with topping.

Cook's tip: Recipe can be baked in a greased and lined 1¹/₂ x 7 x 11 in/4 x 18 x 28 cm cake pan, if desired.

COUNTRY PEAR CAKE

Serves 6
Oven temperature 350°F, 180°C

2 eggs

³/₄ cup/185 g sugar

¹/₃ cup/90 mL milk

1¹/₂ cups/185 g self-rising flour, sifted

¹/₄ cup/30 g dried bread crumbs

2 pears, cored, peeled and sliced

2 tablespoons/30 g butter

¹/₂ cup/60 g sliced almonds

1   Place eggs and sugar in a bowl and beat until light and fluffy. Fold milk and flour, alternately, into egg mixture.

2   Sprinkle bread crumbs into the bottom of a 3 in/7.5 cm deep, greased and lined 9 in/23 cm round cake pan. Spoon half the batter into pan and arrange pear slices on top. Spoon remaining batter over pears, dot with butter and sprinkle with almonds. Bake for 30-35 minutes or until cooked when tested with a skewer. Allow to stand in pan for 10 minutes before turning onto a wire rack to cool.

Cook's tip: Recipe can be baked in a greased and floured 7 x 11 in/18 x 28 cm cake pan, if desired.

DUNDEE CAKE

Makes a deep 8 in/20 cm round cake
Oven temperature 300°F, 150°C

1 cup/2 sticks/250 g butter, softened

1 teaspoon rum extract

1 cup/220 g superfine sugar

4 eggs, lightly beaten

2 cups/250 g flour

1 teaspoon baking powder

¹/₄ cup/30 g cornstarch

1¹/₂ cups/250 g golden seedless raisins

1²/₃ cups/250 g currants

³/₄ cup/125 g diced mixed candied citrus peel

1 cup/125 g slivered almonds

¹/₃ cup/60 g candied cherries, halved

2 teaspoons finely grated orange rind

1 tablespoon orange juice

¹/₃ cup/45 g blanched almonds

1   Place butter and rum extract into a large bowl and beat until light and fluffy. Gradually add sugar, beating well until mixture is creamy.

2   Add eggs one at a time, beating well after each addition. Sift together flour, baking powder and cornstarch, then fold into butter mixture.

3   Stir in raisins, currants, mixed peel, slivered almonds, cherries, orange rind and orange juice. Spoon mixture into a 3 in/7.5 cm deep, greased and lined 8 in/20 cm round cake pan or springform pan. Decorate top of cake with almonds, arranged in circles, and bake for 2¹/₂-3 hours, or until cooked when tested with a skewer. Cool cake in pan before turning out.

1   Place butter or shortening and ³/₄ cup/170 g of the sugar in a bowl and beat until light and fluffy. Add egg and beat well.

2   Sift together flour and baking soda. Stir flour mixture into butter mixture. Turn dough onto a lightly floured surface and knead briefly. Wrap dough in plastic wrap and refrigerate for 30 minutes or until firm.

3   Place cinnamon and remaining sugar in a small bowl and mix to combine. Roll dough into small balls, then roll balls in sugar mixture and place 2 in/5 cm apart on lightly greased baking sheets and bake for 8 minutes or until golden. Remove from oven and transfer to wire racks to cool.

Cook's tip: Fat or shortening in whatever form makes a baked product tender and helps to improve its keeping quality. In most baked goods, top quality margarine and butter are interchangeable.

CINNAMON CRISPS

Makes 25
Oven temperature 350°F, 180°C

¹/₂ cup/1 stick/125 g butter or shortening

1 cup/220 g superfine sugar

1 egg

1¹/₂ cups/185 g flour

¹/₂ teaspoon baking soda

2 teaspoons ground cinnamon

MINI APRICOT TURNOVERS

1   To make filling, place apricots, hazelnuts (filberts), ginger, packed brown sugar and pie spice in a bowl and mix to combine.

2   Cut out sixteen rounds from pastry sheets using a 4 in/10 cm cutter. Place a spoonful of filling in the center of each pastry round. Brush edges with a little water, fold pastry over to form a half circle and press together using a fork to seal and make a decorative edge. Brush each turnover with milk and sprinkle with a little granulated brown (raw or demerara) sugar. Place turnovers on wet baking sheets and bake for 12-15 minutes or until puffed and golden.

Variation: You might like to try making these with canned peaches or apples instead of apricots.

Makes 16
Oven temperature 425°F, 220°C

1¹/₂ lb/750 g prerolled frozen puff pastry sheets, thawed

1 tablespoon water

1 tablespoon milk

1 tablespoon granulated brown (raw or demerara) sugar

APRICOT FILLING
14 oz/440 g canned apricots, drained and sliced

2 oz/60 g chopped hazelnuts (filberts), toasted

3 tablespoons/45 g crystallized ginger, chopped

2 tablespoons packed brown sugar

1 teaspoon pumpkin pie spice

GOLDEN WAFFLES

Makes 16 waffles

3 cups/375 g flour

4 teaspoons baking powder

1 teaspoon salt

¹/₄ cup/60 g superfine sugar

2¹/₄ cups/560 mL milk

3 eggs, separated

¹/₂ cup/1 stick/125 g butter or shortening, melted

1   Sift flour, baking powder and salt together into a bowl. Stir in sugar.

2   Whisk together milk, egg yolks and butter or shortening. Make a well in center of flour mixture and mix in milk mixture until just combined. Place egg whites in a bowl and beat until stiff peaks form, then fold into batter. Do not overmix.

3   Cook batter in a preheated, greased waffle iron following the manufacturer's instructions. Serve waffles hot with topping of your choice.

Brown Sugar Waffles: Use packed brown sugar in place of superfine sugar.

Citrus Waffles: Mix 1 teaspoon finely grated orange or lemon rind into batter.

Banana Waffles: Mash ¹/₂ banana and mix into batter before folding in egg whites.

Freeze it: Waffles can be frozen in an airtight freezer bag or container, then reheated in the oven or toaster straight from the freezer.

Below: Golden Waffles
Right: Eggless Gingerbread (page 71), Ginger Crunch (page 71), Shortbread Swirls (page 70)

WHOLEWHEAT HERMITS

Makes 20
Oven temperature 350°F, 180°C

2 cups/315 g wholewheat flour, sifted and grits returned

³/₄ teaspoon baking soda

¹/₂ teaspoon ground cinnamon

¹/₃ cup/90 g granulated brown (raw or demerara) sugar

¹/₂ cup/1 stick/125 g butter or shortening

³/₄ cup/125 g chopped raisins

¹/₂ cup/30 g chopped dried apples

1 egg, lightly beaten

¹/₃ cup/90 mL milk

1 Place flour, soda, cinnamon and sugar in a large bowl. Cut in butter or shortening. Stir in raisins and apples, then gradually add egg and enough milk to make a thick dough.

2 Place large spoonfuls of dough on greased baking sheets and bake for 12-15 minutes, or until cooked and golden brown.

GRANOLA BARS

Makes 24
Oven temperature 325°F, 160°C

¹/₄ cup/¹/₂ stick/60 g butter

¹/₄ cup/90 g honey

2 eggs, lightly beaten

1 cup/200 g plain yogurt

8 oz/250 g ricotta cheese

¹/₂ cup/45 g grated dry coconut

¹/₃ cup/45 g sliced almonds

³/₄ cup/125 g chopped raisins

1 cup/155 g wholewheat flour, sifted and grits returned

4 tablespoons sesame seeds

1 Place butter and honey in a mixing bowl and beat to combine. Gradually mix in eggs and yogurt, then stir in ricotta cheese, coconut, almonds, raisins, flour and sesame seeds.

2 Pour mixture into a shallow, greased and lined 7 x 11 in/ 18 x 28 cm cake pan and bake for 35-40 minutes or until firm and golden brown. Cool layer in pan, then cut into bars.

SHORTBREAD SWIRLS

Makes 40
Oven temperature 375°F, 190°C

¹/₂ cup/1 stick/125 g butter, chopped

³/₄ cup/125 g confectioners' sugar

1¹/₂ cups/185 g flour

¹/₃ cup/90 g dairy sour cream

4 teaspoons lemon juice

2 teaspoons finely grated lemon rind

1 Place butter, confectioners' sugar, flour, sour cream, lemon juice and lemon rind in a food processor and process until smooth.

2 Spoon dough into a pastry bag fitted with a large star tube and pipe swirls of mixture onto greased baking sheets. Bake for 10-12 minutes or until lightly golden. Cool cookies on sheets. Dust with confectioners' sugar.

Orange Swirls: Replace lemon juice and lemon rind with orange juice and orange rind.

GINGER CRUNCH

Makes 30

¹/₂ cup/1 stick/125 g butter or shortening

³/₄ cup/185 g sugar

¹/₂ cup/125 mL sweetened condensed milk

4 teaspoons light molasses

2¹/₄ cups/250 g crisp gingersnap cookie crumbs

2 oz/60 g pecans, finely chopped

2 tablespoons finely chopped crystallized ginger or preserved ginger in syrup

1 Place butter or shortening, sugar, condensed milk and molasses in a small saucepan and cook over a medium heat, stirring constantly, until mixture is smooth. Bring to the boil, then reduce heat and simmer for 3-4 minutes or until mixture thickens slightly.

2 Place cookie crumbs, pecans and ginger in a bowl, pour in condensed milk mixture and mix well to combine. Press mixture into a shallow, greased and lined 9 in/23 cm square cake pan and refrigerate until set. Cut into bars.

EGGLESS GINGERBREAD

Makes an 8 in/20 cm ring cake
Oven temperature 350°F, 180°C

¹/₂ cup/1 stick/125 g butter or shortening, melted

¹/₂ cup/125 mL hot water

¹/₂ cup/170 g light molasses, warmed

1¹/₂ cups/185 g flour, sifted

³/₄ teaspoon baking soda

4 teaspoons ground ginger

¹/₂ teaspoon ground nutmeg

¹/₂ cup/90 g packed brown sugar

2 tablespoons grated dry coconut

LEMON FROSTING
1¹/₂ cups/230 g confectioners' sugar, sifted

1 tablespoon/15 g butter, softened

2 teaspoons lemon juice

milk

1 Place butter, water and light molasses in a large bowl and mix to combine. Stir in flour, baking soda, ginger, nutmeg and sugar and mix to combine.

2 Spoon batter into a 3 in/7.5 cm deep, greased 8 in/20 cm ring pan and bake for 35-40 minutes or until cake is cooked when tested with a skewer. Stand cake in pan for 5 minutes before turning onto a wire rack to cool.

3 To make frosting, place confectioners' sugar in a mixing bowl, mix in butter, lemon juice and enough milk to make frosting with an easy-to-spread consistency. Spread over cold cake and sprinkle with coconut.

Cook's tip: Recipe can be baked in an 8 in/20 cm greased and floured springform pan, or 2 in/5 cm deep, 9 in/23 cm square pan, if desired.

SPEEDY DATE BARS

Makes 24
Oven temperature 350°F, 180°C

¹/₃ cup/90 g butter or shortening

³/₄ cup/185 g granulated brown (raw or demerara) sugar

1 egg

1 cup/155 g chopped dried dates

1 cup/125 g flour, sifted with ¹/₂ teaspoon baking powder

¹/₂ cup/60 g granola

2 tablespoons sunflower seeds

1 tablespoon poppy seeds

2 tablespoons chopped pumpkin seeds

¹/₂ cup/100 g plain yogurt

LEMON GLAZE
1 tablespoon/15 g butter

2 tablespoons hot water

¹/₃ cup/90 mL lemon juice

2 cups/350 g confectioners' sugar, sifted

1 Place butter or shortening and sugar in a small bowl and beat until light and fluffy. Beat in egg, then stir in dates, sifted flour, granola, sunflower seeds, poppy seeds, pumpkin seeds and yogurt.

2 Spoon batter into a shallow, greased and lined 7 x 11 in/ 18 x 28 cm cake pan and bake for 25 minutes, or until firm and golden brown. Cool in pan.

3 To make glaze, melt butter in hot water and stir in lemon juice. Add confectioners' sugar and beat until smooth. Spread glaze evenly over cold layer. Allow glaze to set, then cut into fingers, bars or squares.

OATY COOKIES

Makes 15
Oven temperature 350°F, 180°C

¹/₄ cup/¹/₂ stick/60 g butter or shortening

3 tablespoons packed brown sugar

1 teaspoon vanilla

1 egg

¹/₂ cup/75 g wholewheat flour

¹/₄ teaspoon baking soda

1 cup/90 g rolled oats

4 tablespoons wheat germ

4 tablespoons chopped pecans

4 tablespoons chopped dates

PINK GLAZE
1 tablespoon/15 g butter

3 tablespoons hot water

1 cup/155 g confectioners' sugar, sifted

few drops pink food coloring

1 Place butter or shortening in a small bowl and beat until light and fluffy. Beat in sugar and vanilla. Add egg and beat to combine.

2 Sift together wholewheat flour and baking soda, stir into egg mixture, returning grits to bowl. Stir in oats, wheat germ, pecans and dates.

3 Place spoonfuls of mixture on lightly greased baking sheets and bake for 10 minutes or until golden brown. Remove from oven and transfer cookies to wire racks to cool.

4 To make glaze, place butter and hot water in a bowl. Add confectioners' sugar and beat until smooth. Color with food coloring and place a drop of glaze on each cookie.

Wholewheat Hermits (page 70), Speedy Date Bars, Oaty Cookies, Granola Bars (page 70)

Rich Fruit Cake

Makes a deep 8 in/20 cm round cake
Oven temperature 300°F, 150°C

1¹/₂ cups/250 g golden seedless raisins

1²/₃ cups/250 g currants

1¹/₂ cups/250 g seeded raisins

³/₄ cup/125 g diced mixed candied citrus peel

1¹/₃ cups/250 g candied cherries, chopped

¹/₃ cup/60 g candied pineapple, chopped

¹/₃ cup/60 g pitted dried dates, chopped

¹/₂ cup/125 mL brandy

1 cup/2 sticks/250 g butter, softened

1 cup/170 g packed brown sugar

5 eggs

2 oz/60 g semi-sweet cooking chocolate, melted and cooled

1 teaspoon vanilla

1 teaspoon almond extract

2 tablespoons raspberry jam

1 teaspoon finely grated lemon rind

2 tablespoons lemon juice

2 cups/250 g flour

1 teaspoon pumpkin pie spice

1 teaspoon ground ginger

¹/₄ teaspoon salt

FRUIT AND NUT TOPPING
2 tablespoons apricot jam

1 cup/90 g pecan or walnut halves

¹/₂ cup/90 g brazil nuts

¹/₃ cup/60 g blanched almonds

¹/₃ cup/60 g red candied cherries

¹/₃ cup/60 g green candied cherries

1   Place golden raisins, currants, raisins, mixed peel, chopped cherries, pineapple and dates in a bowl. Pour over 4 tablespoons brandy and toss to combine. Cover and stand overnight.

2   Lightly grease a 3 in/7.5 cm deep, 8 in/20 cm round or square cake pan or round springform pan and line bottom and sides of pan with brown paper, then with parchment or waxed paper.

3   Place butter in a large bowl and beat until light and fluffy. Gradually add brown sugar, beating well. Add eggs one at a time, beating well after each addition. Stir in chocolate, vanilla, almond extract, jam, lemon rind and lemon juice.

4   Sift together flour, pie spice, ginger and salt. Stir flour mixture and fruit mixture, alternately, into butter mixture and mix well to combine.

5   Spoon batter into prepared pan and smooth top. Drop pan onto a flat surface to break up any air bubbles, then cook for 3-3¹/₂ hours or until cooked when tested with a skewer. Remove cake from oven, sprinkle with remaining brandy and set aside to cool in pan. When completely cold remove cake from pan. If you are planning to store the cake, leave the paper on, wrap cake in a double thickness of aluminum foil and store in an airtight container.

6   To decorate, place jam in a small saucepan and heat over a low heat, stirring, until melted, then push through a sieve. Brush top of cake with warm jam and then, using the picture on page 76 as a guide, arrange pecans or walnuts, brazil nuts, almonds and cherries in an attractive pattern.

Cook's tip: To line the cake pan, use a double-thickness folded strip of brown paper 2 in/5 cm higher than the cake pan and long enough to fit around the pan to overlap by about 1 in/2.5 cm. On the folded edge turn up about 1 in/2.5 cm and crease, then using scissors snip at regular intervals across the margin as far as the crease. Cut a piece of parchment paper in the same way. Cut out a piece of brown paper and a piece of parchment paper to fit in the bottom of the pan. Grease the pan and place the strip of brown paper inside the pan with the snipped margin lying flat on the bottom. Ensure that the ends overlap so that the sides are completely covered by the paper. Repeat the process using the strip of parchment paper. Place the bottom piece of brown paper, then the parchment paper in the pan to cover the snipped margin. Make sure that the paper fits neatly into the pan.

1   Place rice cereal, bran flakes, almonds, apricots, pineapple, ginger, seeded and golden seedless raisins in a large bowl and set aside.

2   Place butter, cream, honey and sugar in a saucepan and cook over a low heat, stirring constantly, until sugar dissolves and butter melts. Bring to the boil, then reduce heat and simmer for 5 minutes or until mixture thickens slightly.

3   Pour honey mixture into dry ingredients and mix well to combine. Press mixture into a shallow, greased and lined 7 x 11 in/18 x 28 cm cake pan. Refrigerate until firm, then cut into squares.

1   Place butter or shortening and sugar in a bowl and beat until light and fluffy. Add eggs one at a time, beating well after each addition.

2   Sift flour, cinnamon and cloves together into a bowl. Mix in almonds. Add flour mixture to butter mixture and mix to combine.

3   Spoon half the batter into a 3 in/7.5 cm deep, greased and lined 8 in/20 cm square cake pan. Spread with 4 tablespoons jam and top with remaining batter. Bake for 1 hour or until golden and cooked when tested with a skewer. Stand cake in pan for 5 minutes before turning onto a wire rack to cool. Spread top of cold cake with remaining jam and decorate with whipped cream and cherries.

Cook's tip: Recipe can be baked in greased and paper-lined 8 in/20 cm round springform pan, if desired.

FRUITY CEREAL SQUARES

Makes 30

3 oz/90 g unsweetened crisp rice cereal

1 cup/45 g bran flake cereal, crumbled

1 cup/125 g slivered almonds, toasted

1 cup/125 g dried apricots, chopped

$^1/_2$ cup/100 g candied pineapple, chopped

$^1/_2$ cup/100 g crystallized ginger or preserved ginger in syrup, chopped

$^1/_2$ cup/90 g seeded raisins, chopped

1 cup/170 g golden seedless raisins

$^1/_2$ cup/1 stick/125 g butter

$^1/_2$ cup/125 mL whipping cream

$^1/_2$ cup/170 g honey

$^1/_3$ cup/90 g granulated brown (raw or demerara) sugar

CHERRY ALMOND CAKE

Makes a deep 8 in/20 cm square cake
Oven temperature 350°F, 180°C

1 cup/2 sticks/250 g butter or shortening

1 cup/220 g superfine sugar

2 eggs

2 cups/250 g flour

$^1/_2$ teaspoon ground cinnamon

$^1/_2$ teaspoon ground cloves

$2^1/_4$ cups/250 g ground almonds

7 tablespoons cherry jam

TO DECORATE
candied cherries

whipped cream

DATE BARS

Makes 30
Oven temperature 350°F, 180°C

³/₄ cup/185 mL evaporated milk

³/₄ cup/125 g pitted dates, chopped

¹/₂ cup/1 stick/125 g butter, softened

1 teaspoon vanilla

¹/₂ cup/100 g superfine sugar

**1 cup/125 g flour, sifted
with ¹/₂ teaspoon baking powder**

²/₃ cup/60 g pecans, chopped

1   Place milk in a saucepan and cook over a low heat until just boiling, then remove pan from heat. Place dates in a bowl, pour hot milk over and set aside to cool.

2   Place butter, vanilla and sugar in a large bowl and beat until light and fluffy. Mix sifted flour and date mixture, alternately, into butter mixture, then fold in pecans. Spoon batter into a greased and lined 9 in/23 cm square or 7 x 11 in/18 x 28 cm baking pan and bake for 25-30 minutes or until firm. Stand in pan 5 minutes before turning onto a wire rack to cool. Cut into bars.

Below: Rich Fruit Cake (page 74)
Right: Fruity Cereal Squares (page 75), Date Bars

DATE WRAPS

Makes 20
Oven temperature 325°F, 160°C

20 dried dates, pitted

4 tablespoons brandy

Ingredients for Basic Drop Cookies recipe (see below)

1   Soak dates in brandy for 30 minutes, then drain.

2   Make up Basic Drop Cookies as described in recipe. Divide cookie dough into 20 equal portions. Mold each portion around a date. Place on greased baking sheets and bake for 20-25 minutes, or until golden brown. Stand on sheets for 5 minutes before transferring to wire racks to cool.

BASIC DROP COOKIES

Makes 40
Oven temperature 350°F, 180°C

$^1/_2$ cup/1 stick/125 g butter or shortening

$^3/_4$ cup/170 g superfine sugar

1 teaspoon vanilla

1 egg

2 cups/250 g flour, sifted with $^3/_4$ teaspoon baking soda

1   Place butter or shortening, sugar and vanilla in a bowl and beat until light and fluffy. Add egg and beat well. Fold in sifted flour, cover and refrigerate for 2 hours.

2   Roll heaped teaspoons of mixture into balls. Place on greased baking sheets, spacing well apart to allow for spreading. Flatten each cookie slightly with a fork and bake for 12-15 minutes or until golden brown. Stand on sheets for 5 minutes before transferring to wire racks to cool.

Spicy Fruit Cookies: Replace 5 tablespoons of the superfine sugar with 5 tablespoons packed brown sugar. Sift 2 teaspoons of cinnamon, 1 teaspoon of pumpkin pie spice and 1 teaspoon of ginger with the flour. Roll out mixture and cut 16 rounds with a cookie cutter. Place a teaspoon of bottled fruit mincemeat on half the rounds and cover with remaining rounds. Press the edges lightly to seal and bake at 350°F/180°C for 20-25 minutes, or until golden brown.

Three-Chocolate Cookies: Add $1^1/_2$ oz/45 g finely chopped semi-sweet cooking chocolate, $1^1/_2$ oz/45 g finely chopped milk chocolate and $1^1/_2$ oz/45 g finely chopped white chocolate to the cookie mixture after beating in the egg. Roll teaspoons of mixture into balls. Place on greased baking sheets. Flatten slightly and bake at 350°F/180°C for 12-15 minutes or until golden brown.

Creamy Jam Drops: Roll teaspoons of mixture into balls. Place on greased baking sheets and flatten slightly. Make an indent in the center of each round and fill with a small amount of cream cheese and top with a little jam of your choice. Be careful not to fill the holes too much, or the jam will overflow during cooking. Bake at 350°F/180°C for 12-15 minutes, or until golden brown. Stand on sheets for 5 minutes before transferring to wire racks to cool.

1   Place egg whites in a bowl and beat until stiff peaks form. Fold in sugar, hazelnuts (filberts) and flour.

2   Place teaspoons of mixture 1 in/2.5 cm apart on greased baking sheets and bake for 12-15 minutes or until lightly browned. Stand on sheets for 5 minutes before transferring to wire racks to cool. Sandwich cold cookies together with hazelnut spread.

HAZELNUT GEMS

Makes 25
Oven temperature 350°F, 180°C

3 egg whites

³/₄ cup/170 g superfine sugar

4 oz/125 g hazelnuts (filberts), ground

¹/₄ cup/30 g flour

¹/₂ cup/125 g bottled chocolate hazelnut spread

LIGHT FRUIT CAKE

Makes a deep 8 in/20 cm round cake
Oven temperature 350°F, 180°C

1   Place raisins, 1 cup/185 g of the cherries and lemon rind in a bowl, pour over ¹/₂ cup/125 mL of the brandy and mix to combine. Cover and stand overnight.

2   Place butter in a bowl and beat until light and fluffy. Gradually add sugar, beating well. Add egg yolks one at a time, beating well after each addition.

3   Sift together flour, baking powder, pie spice and cinnamon. Fold flour mixture and fruit mixture, alternately, into butter mixture.

4   Place egg whites in a clean bowl and beat until soft peaks form. Fold egg white mixture into fruit mixture. Spoon batter into a 3 in/7.5 cm deep, greased and lined 8 in/20 cm round cake pan or springform pan and smooth top with a spatula. Arrange almonds and remaining cherries decoratively on top of cake and bake for 1¹/₂ hours or until cooked when tested with a skewer. Using a skewer, pierce the cake several times then sprinkle with remaining brandy. Wrap cake in a teatowel and set aside to cool completely before turning out.

Cook's tip: To prevent dried fruit from sinking to the bottom of a cake, toss the fruit in a tablespoon of the flour used in the recipe before adding to the cake batter.

1 cup/185 g golden seedless raisins

1¹/₄ cups/220 g candied cherries, halved

1 tablespoon finely grated lemon rind

³/₄ cup/185 mL brandy

³/₄ cup/1¹/₂ sticks/185 g butter

³/₄ cup/185 g sugar

4 eggs, separated

2¹/₂ cups/315 g flour

1 teaspoon baking powder

1 teaspoon pumpkin pie spice

¹/₂ teaspoon ground cinnamon

¹/₃ cup/60 g blanched almonds

FROSTED NUT SQUARES

Makes 30 squares

2¹⁄₄ cups/250 g plain cookie crumbs

¹⁄₂ cup/90 g packed brown sugar

1 oz/30 g macadamia or brazil nuts, chopped

2 tablespoons cocoa powder

1 teaspoon coffee extract (chicory)

¹⁄₄ cup/60 mL milk

¹⁄₂ cup/1 stick/125 g butter, melted

CHOCOLATE FROSTING
4 oz/125 g semi-sweet cooking chocolate, broken into small pieces

¹⁄₃ cup/90 g unsalted (sweet) butter

1 Place cookie crumbs, sugar, nuts, cocoa powder, coffee extract (chicory), milk and butter in a bowl and mix well to combine. Press mixture into a shallow, greased and lined 7 x 11 in/18 x 28 cm cake pan and refrigerate until firm.

2 To make frosting, place chocolate and butter in a small saucepan and cook over a low heat, stirring constantly, until melted and combined. Spread over layer in cake pan and refrigerate until set. Cut into squares.

Cook's tip: If coffee extract (chicory) is unavailable, substitute with 2 teaspoons instant coffee powder dissolved in 2 teaspoons boiling water.

LEMON AND PISTACHIO NUT BARS

Makes 30

2¹⁄₄ cups/250 g plain cookie crumbs

3 oz/90 g pistachio nuts, chopped

2 teaspoons finely grated lemon rind

¹⁄₂ cup/125 mL sweetened condensed milk

¹⁄₂ cup/1 stick/125 g butter, melted

LEMON PISTACHIO TOPPING
4 oz/125 g cream cheese, softened

¹⁄₂ cup/90 g confectioners' sugar, sifted

2 teaspoons lemon juice

¹⁄₄ cup/45 g diced mixed candied citrus peel, finely chopped

1 tablespoon chopped pistachio nuts

1 Place cookie crumbs, nuts, lemon rind, condensed milk and butter in a bowl and mix to combine. Press mixture into a shallow, greased and lined 7 x 11 in/18 x 28 cm cake pan and refrigerate until firm.

2 To make topping, place cream cheese and confectioners' sugar in a mixing bowl and beat until light and fluffy. Beat in lemon juice and spread over mixture in cake pan. Sprinkle with mixed peel and nuts. Refrigerate until topping is firm, then cut into bars.

Hazelnut Gems (page 79), Frosted Nut Squares, Lemon and Pistachio Nut Bars

SPICED GINGER DROPS

Makes 30
Oven temperature 350°F, 180°C

1 cup/125 g flour

¼ teaspoon ground ginger

¼ teaspoon pumpkin pie spice

¼ teaspoon ground cinnamon

½ teaspoon baking soda

¼ cup/½ stick/60 g butter or shortening, cut into pieces

½ cup/90 g packed brown sugar

2½ tablespoons light molasses, warmed

1½ tablespoons finely chopped crystallized ginger or preserved ginger in syrup

1   Sift flour, ground ginger, pie spice, cinnamon and baking soda together into a large bowl. Cut in butter or shortening until mixture resembles fine bread crumbs. Stir in sugar, molasses and crystallized ginger.

2   Turn onto a lightly floured surface and knead to form a soft dough. Roll heaped teaspoons of mixture into balls and place 1¼ in/3 cm apart on greased baking sheets. Bake for 10-15 minutes or until golden. Remove from oven and transfer to wire racks to cool.

Below: Spiced Ginger Drops
Right: Fig Pinwheels (page 84)

PEAR AND HONEY CAKE

Makes a 7 x 11 in/18 x 28 cm cake
Oven temperature 350°F, 180°C

¹/₂ cup/1 stick/125 g butter or shortening

¹/₃ cup/90 g sugar

2 tablespoons honey

2 eggs

1 cup/125 g flour

1 teaspoon baking powder

¹/₂ teaspoon ground cinnamon

¹/₄ cup/60 mL milk

PEAR AND HONEY TOPPING
²/₃ cup/90 g dried apricots

boiling water

28 oz/810 g canned pear halves, drained and cut in half lengthwise

¹/₃ cup/125 g honey, warmed

1   To make topping, place apricots in a small bowl and pour over enough boiling water to cover. Set aside to soak for 15 minutes, then drain and pat dry with paper towels.

2   Arrange pears and apricots decoratively over the bottom of a shallow, greased 7 x 11 in/18 x 28 cm cake pan. Pour honey over fruit and set aside.

3   Place butter or shortening in a bowl and beat until soft. Add sugar and honey and continue beating until mixture is light and creamy. Add eggs, one at a time beating well after each addition.

4   Sift together flour, baking powder and cinnamon. Fold flour mixture and milk, alternately, into butter mixture. Spoon batter carefully over fruit, smoothing the top to level and bake for 30-35 minutes or until cake is cooked when tested with a skewer. Stand cake in pan for 5 minutes before turning onto a wire rack to cool. Serve cake warm or cold.

FIG PINWHEELS

Makes 50
Oven temperature 350°F, 180°C

³/₄ cup/1¹/₂ sticks/185 g butter

1 cup/170 g packed brown sugar

1 egg

¹/₂ teaspoon vanilla

3 cups/375 g flour

¹/₂ teaspoon baking soda

¹/₄ teaspoon ground cinnamon

¹/₄ teaspoon ground nutmeg

2 tablespoons milk

FIG AND ALMOND FILLING
1¹/₂ cups/250 g dried figs, finely chopped

¹/₄ cup/60 g sugar

¹/₂ cup/125 mL water

¹/₄ teaspoon pumpkin pie spice

¹/₄ cup/30 g almonds, finely chopped

1   To make filling, place figs, sugar, water and pie spice in a saucepan and bring to the boil. Reduce heat and cook, stirring for 2-3 minutes or until mixture is thick. Remove pan from heat and stir in almonds. Set aside to cool.

2   Place butter in a large bowl and beat until light and fluffy. Gradually add sugar, beating well until mixture is creamy. Beat in egg and vanilla.

3   Sift together flour, baking soda, cinnamon and nutmeg. Beat milk and half the flour mixture into butter mixture. Stir in remaining flour mixture. Turn dough onto a lightly floured surface and knead lightly. Roll into a ball, wrap in plastic wrap and refrigerate for 30 minutes.

4   Divide dough into two portions. Roll one portion out to an 8 x 11 in/20 x 28 cm rectangle and spread with half the filling. Roll up from the long side, like a jelly roll. Repeat with remaining dough and filling. Wrap rolls in plastic wrap and refrigerate for 15 minutes or until you are ready to cook the cookies.

5   Cut rolls into ¹/₂ in/1 cm slices. Place slices on greased baking sheets and bake for 10-12 minutes. Stand cookies on sheets for 1 minute before transferring to wire racks to cool.

BANANA LOAF WITH MAPLE ICING

1 Place butter or shortening in a bowl and beat until light and creamy. Add sugar, vanilla and bananas and continue beating until mixture is light and fluffy. Add 2 tablespoons of the sifted flour and beat well to combine.

2 Add eggs, one at a time, beating well after each addition. Fold yogurt and remaining flour, alternately, into banana mixture. Spoon batter into a greased and lined 4½ x 8½ in/11 x 21 cm loaf pan and bake for 1 hour or until cooked when tested with a skewer. Stand in pan for 5 minutes before turning onto a wire rack to cool.

3 To make glaze, place butter in a bowl and beat until light and creamy. Add confectioners' sugar and maple syrup and continue beating until glaze is smooth. Spread cold loaf with glaze and top with sliced banana, if desired.

Makes a 4½ x 8½ in/11 x 21 cm loaf
Oven temperature 350°F, 180°C

½ cup/1 stick/125 g butter or shortening

¾ cup/170 g superfine sugar

½ teaspoon vanilla

3 medium, very ripe bananas, peeled and coarsely mashed

2 cups/250 g flour, sifted with ½ teaspoon baking soda

2 eggs

½ cup/100 g plain yogurt

MAPLE GLAZE
3 tablespoons/45 g butter

¾ cup/125 g confectioners' sugar, sifted

2 teaspoons maple syrup

1 banana, sliced (optional)

FRUITY CARROT LOAF

1 Sift wholewheat flour, rye flour, salt, baking soda and cinnamon together into a bowl. Add sugar, pineapple, carrot, eggs, oil and vanilla and beat until well combined. Stir walnuts into carrot mixture.

2 Spoon batter into a greased and lined 4½ x 8½ in/11 x 21 cm loaf pan and bake for 25-30 minutes or until cooked when tested with a skewer. Stand in pan for 5 minutes before turning out onto a wire rack to cool.

Cook's tip: For a festive-looking loaf you might like to decorate the top with marzipan (almond paste) carrots. To make carrots, knead 4 oz/125 g marzipan (almond paste) with orange food coloring until pliable and evenly colored. Dust hands lightly with cornstarch, then pull off small pieces of marzipan and form into carrot shapes. Use a skewer to mark the grooves. Decorate top of carrots with a sprig of fresh dill weed. Keep marzipan covered with a damp cloth to prevent drying while making each carrot.

Makes a 4½ x 8½ in/11 x 21 cm loaf
Oven temperature 350°F, 180°C

1 cup/155 g wholewheat flour

½ cup/60 g rye flour

½ teaspoon salt

¾ teaspoon baking soda

1 teaspoon ground cinnamon

½ cup/125 g granulated brown (raw or demerara) sugar

5 oz/155 g crushed pineapple, undrained

1 carrot, shredded

2 eggs

½ cup/125 mL vegetable oil

1 teaspoon vanilla

½ cup/60 g chopped walnuts

SPECIAL OCCASION CAKES

A fabulous homemade cake is the
perfect way to celebrate a special occasion.
Some of the cakes in this section are quick and
easy to make, while others take a little more
time to prepare, but are well worth the effort.

Layered Orange and Almond Gâteau (page 88)

LAYERED ORANGE AND ALMOND GATEAU

Serves 10
Oven temperature 350°F, 180°C

3 eggs

1 cup/220 g superfine sugar

1 tablespoon orange juice

1 tablespoon finely grated orange rind

1¾ cups/220 g flour

¼ cup/30 g cornstarch

1½ teaspoons baking powder

1 teaspoon baking soda

1 cup/250 g dairy sour cream, lightly beaten

1 cup/2 sticks/250 g butter, melted and cooled

GRAND MARNIER SYRUP
½ cup/125 g sugar

¼ cup/60 mL orange juice

¼ cup/60 mL orange-flavored liqueur

ORANGE BUTTER CREAM
½ cup/125 g sugar

½ cup/125 mL water

4 egg yolks

1 cup/2 sticks/250 g unsalted (sweet) butter

2 teaspoons finely grated orange rind

¼ cup/60 mL orange juice

2 tablespoons orange-flavored liqueur

2½ oz/75 g sliced almonds, toasted

1   Place eggs, sugar, orange juice and orange rind in a large bowl and beat until thick and creamy. Sift together flour, cornstarch, baking powder and baking soda. Place sour cream and butter in a small bowl and whisk lightly to combine. Fold flour mixture and sour cream mixture, alternately, into egg mixture.

2   Spoon batter into three lightly greased and lined 9 in/ 23 cm round layer pans and bake for 15-20 minutes or until cooked when tested with a skewer.

3   Make syrup five minutes before cakes complete cooking. Place sugar, orange juice and liqueur in a saucepan and cook, stirring constantly, until sugar dissolves.

4   Turn cakes onto wire racks set on trays. Using a skewer, pierce surface of cakes to make holes that reach about halfway through the cakes. Spoon hot syrup over hot cakes and set aside to cool completely.

5   To make butter cream, place sugar and water in a small saucepan and cook over a medium heat, stirring constantly, until sugar dissolves. Bring syrup to the boil and cook until mixture reaches soft-ball stage (239°F/115°C on a candy thermometer). Beat egg yolks to combine and continue beating while slowly pouring in sugar syrup. Beat for 5 minutes longer or until mixture cools and is of a thick mousse-like consistency. In a separate bowl beat butter until light and creamy, then gradually beat into egg yolk mixture. Beat in orange rind, orange juice and liqueur.

6   To assemble, sandwich layers together with a little butter cream, then spread remaining butter cream over top and sides of cake. Press almonds around sides of cake.

STRAWBERRY SHORTBREAD FAN

1 To make sponge cake, place eggs in a bowl and beat until light and fluffy. Add sugar a little at a time, beating well, until mixture is thick and creamy. Combine milk and butter. Fold flour and milk mixture, alternately, into egg mixture. Pour into a greased and lightly floured 8 in/20 cm round layer pan and bake for 20-25 minutes or until cooked when tested with a skewer. Stand in pan for 5 minutes before turning onto a wire rack to cool.

2 To make Shortbread, place flour, confectioners' sugar and ground rice (rice flour) in a large bowl and mix to combine. Rub in butter, using fingertips, until mixture resembles coarse bread crumbs. Stir in lemon rind and vanilla. Turn dough onto a floured surface and knead until dough is smooth. Roll out to 1/4 in/5 mm thick and using an 8 in/20 cm round cake pan as a guide, cut out a circle. Place on a greased and parchment paper-lined baking sheet. Mark twelve wedges on Shortbread and bake at 325°F/ 160°C for 40 minutes or until lightly browned. Cut into wedges. Cool on baking sheet.

3 Spread one side of each wedge with melted chocolate and set aside until chocolate sets.

4 To make Crème Pâtissière, place egg, egg yolks, flour, cornstarch, sugar and vanilla in a small bowl and whisk to combine. Stir 2 tablespoons of hot milk into egg mixture, then stir egg mixture into remaining milk and cook over a low heat, stirring constantly, until custard thickens. Set aside to cool completely. Fold in whipped cream.

5 To make coulis, place strawberries in a food processor or blender and process until smooth. Add sugar to taste.

6 To assemble, spread sponge cake layer with Crème Pâtissière and arrange shortbread wedges, angled upwards, on sponge with halved strawberries tucked between each wedge. Accompany cake with coulis

Serves 12
Oven temperature 350°F, 180°C

12 strawberries, halved
SPONGE CAKE BASE
2 eggs
1/2 cup/100 g superfine sugar
1/4 cup/60 mL milk, warmed
1 teaspoon butter, melted
1/2 cup/60 g flour, sifted
SHORTBREAD
1 cup/125 g flour, sifted
3 tablespoons/30 g confectioners' sugar, sifted
3 tablespoons/30 g ground rice (rice flour), sifted
1/2 cup/1 stick/125 g butter, cubed
1/2 teaspoon finely grated lemon rind
1/2 teaspoon vanilla
4 oz/125 g semi-sweet cooking chocolate, melted
CREME PATISSIERE
1 egg
2 egg yolks
1 tablespoon flour, sifted
1 tablespoon cornstarch, sifted
1/4 cup/60 g superfine sugar
1 teaspoon vanilla
1 1/4 cups/315 mL milk, scalded
1/2 cup/125 mL whipping cream, whipped
STRAWBERRY COULIS
8 oz/250 g strawberries, hulled and halved
sugar to taste

AUSTRIAN COFFEE TORTE

1 Place egg yolks and sugar in a mixing bowl and beat until thick and creamy. Beat in almonds, vanilla and coffee mixture.

2 Place egg whites in a separate bowl and beat until stiff peaks form. Sift flour over egg yolk mixture and fold in with egg white mixture. Spoon batter into a greased and lined 8 in/20 cm springform pan and bake for 20-25 minutes or until cooked when tested with a skewer. Stand in pan for 10 minutes, before turning onto a wire rack to cool.

3 To make Coffee Cream, place cream in a bowl. Beat in coffee mixture, sugar and liqueur. Cut cold cake in half horizontally and use a little of the Coffee Cream to sandwich halves together. Spread remaining Coffee Cream over top and sides of cake. Decorate top with coffee beans or chocolate dots and grated chocolate. Chill. Serve cut into slices.

Left: Austrian Coffee Torte
Above: Strawberry Shortbread Fan (page 89)

Serves 10
Oven temperature 350°F, 180°C

4 eggs, separated

¹/₄ cup/60 g superfine sugar

¹/₂ cup/45 g ground almonds

¹/₂ teaspoon vanilla

1 tablespoon instant coffee powder dissolved in 1 tablespoon boiling water, cooled

¹/₄ cup/30 g flour

COFFEE CREAM
1 cup/250 mL whipping cream, whipped

1 teaspoon instant coffee powder dissolved in 2 teaspoons boiling water, cooled

1 tablespoon superfine sugar

2 tablespoons coffee-flavored liqueur

chocolate-coated candy coffee beans or chocolate dots

semi-sweet cooking chocolate, finely grated

SWEETHEART GATEAU

Serves 10
Oven temperature 325°F, 160°C

6 egg whites

pinch cream of tartar

1¹⁄₂ cups/330 g superfine sugar

1¹⁄₄ cups/125 g ground hazelnuts (filberts)

CHOCOLATE RASPBERRY FILLING
5 oz/155 g semi-sweet cooking chocolate

2 teaspoons rum

1¹⁄₄ cups/300 mL whipping cream, whipped

1 lb/500 g raspberries

confectioners' sugar

1 Place egg whites and cream of tartar in a large bowl and beat until soft peaks form. Add sugar, a spoonful at a time, beating well after each addition. Continue beating until meringue is stiff and glossy. Fold hazelnuts (filberts) into egg white mixture.

2 Line three baking sheets with parchment paper. Lightly grease paper and dust with cornstarch. Using a heart-shaped cake pan or cardboard cutout as a guide, draw an 8 in/20 cm heart on each sheet.

3 Spoon meringue mixture into a large pastry bag fitted with a plain tube. Pipe meringue mixture within the marked hearts and bake for 1¹⁄₂ hours or until meringue is dry and crisp. Cool meringues on baking sheets.

4 To make filling, place chocolate in top of a double boiler set over simmering water and heat, stirring occasionally, until chocolate melts. Stir in rum and remove from heat. Place one meringue heart on a serving plate, spread with half the chocolate mixture, half the cream and one-third of the raspberries. Top with second meringue heart and repeat layers. Top with third meringue heart and remaining raspberries. Dust lightly with confectioners' sugar.

Cook's tip: Make the meringue layers for this special gâteau up to a week in advance and store in an airtight container.

CASSATA CAKE

1 To make cookie layer, sift flour in a bowl. Cut in butter until mixture resembles fine bread crumbs. Add almonds and brown sugar and work into a soft paste. Press mixture into a shallow, greased and lined 7 x 11 in/18 x 28 cm cake pan. Bake for 20 minutes or until golden. Cool in pan.

2 To make filling, place candied fruit in a bowl and sprinkle with liqueur. Cover and set aside to macerate for 1 hour. Place white chocolate in top of a double boiler set over simmering water and heat, stirring occasionally, until chocolate melts. Remove from heat and set aside to cool.

3 Place butter in a bowl and beat until light and creamy. Add sugar a little at a time, beating well after each addition. Beat in eggs one at a time. Stir in white chocolate and fruit mixture. Spread filling over cookie layer and refrigerate for 2 hours or until firm.

4 To make topping, place cream and liqueur in a bowl and beat until soft peaks form. Fold melted chocolate into cream mixture.

5 Using a serrated knife, cut chilled cookie layer in half lengthwise. Place one half, cookie side down, on a serving plate and spread with half the topping. Top with remaining cookie. Spoon remaining topping into a pastry bag fitted with a fluted tube and pipe a decorative border around edges of cake. Sprinkle with chocolate curls and top with violets. Refrigerate until required. Cut into slices to serve.

Cook's tip: Make the cookie layer up to a week in advance and store in an airtight container. The filling can be made the day before and stored in the refrigerator.

Serves 10
Oven temperature 400°F, 200°C

COOKIE LAYER
1 cup/125 g flour

$^1/_2$ cup/1 stick/125 g unsalted (sweet) butter, softened

5 tablespoons chopped almonds

5 tablespoons packed brown sugar

FRUIT FILLING
6 oz/185 g mixed candied fruits, chopped

1 tablespoon liqueur of your choice

2 oz/60 g white chocolate

$^1/_2$ cup/1 stick/125 g unsalted (sweet) butter

$^3/_4$ cup/170 g superfine sugar

2 eggs

CHOCOLATE TOPPING
1 cup/250 mL whipping cream

2 teaspoons liqueur of your choice (use the same liqueur as for the filling)

4 oz/125 g semi-sweet cooking chocolate, melted and cooled

chocolate curls

crystallized violets

CROQUEMBOUCHE

Serves 25
Oven temperature 500°F, 250°C

PROFITEROLES
2 cups/500 mL water

**¹/₂ cup/1 stick/125 g plus 2 tablespoons/
30 g butter, cut into small pieces**

1¹/₂ cups/185 g flour

8 eggs

CUSTARD FILLING
4 egg yolks

¹/₂ cup/100 g superfine sugar

¹/₂ cup/60 g flour, sifted

2¹/₂ cups/600 mL milk

2 tablespoons orange-flavored liqueur

TOFFEE
1¹/₂ cups/375 mL water

3 cups/750 g sugar

DECORATION
crystallized violets or sugared almonds

1   To make Profiteroles, place water and butter in a saucepan, cover and bring to the boil over a medium heat. Remove pan from heat, remove cover and add flour all at once. Using a wooden spoon beat mixture well, return pan to heat and stir until mixture is smooth and leaves the sides of the pan. Remove pan from heat and set aside to cool slightly.

2   Add eggs one at a time, beating well after each addition until light and glossy. Place heaped teaspoons of mixture onto greased baking sheets and bake for 10 minutes. Reduce oven temperature to 350°F/180°C and bake for 15-20 minutes longer or until puffs are golden and crisp.

3   Remove from oven and make small slits in sides of puffs to allow steam to escape. Return to oven for a few minutes to dry out. Place puffs on wire racks to cool.

4   To make filling, place egg yolks and sugar in a bowl and beat until thick and creamy. Fold in flour and 1 tablespoon milk. Place remaining milk in a saucepan and bring to the boil over a medium heat. Stir a little hot milk into egg mixture, then gradually stir egg mixture into hot milk. Cook filling over a low heat, stirring constantly, for 5 minutes or until mixture thickens. Remove pan from heat and set aside to cool slightly. Stir in liqueur and set aside to cool completely. Spoon filling into a pastry bag fitted with a plain tube and pipe a little filling into each puff.

5   To make Toffee, place half the water and half the sugar in a heavy-based saucepan and cook over a low heat, stirring constantly, until sugar dissolves. Increase heat, bring to the boil and boil toffee until golden.

6   To assemble, place a croquembouche cone on a large serving plate. Dip the base of each puff in toffee and arrange in layers around the cone. Place violets or almonds between puffs. Use remaining water and sugar to make a second quantity of toffee. Remove toffee from heat and set aside to cool slightly. Using two wooden spoons spin toffee over and around Croquembouche. Place in a cool place until required. Serve within six hours or the toffee will soften.

Cook's tip: To spin toffee, coat the back of two wooden spoons with the toffee, place them back to back and gently pull apart. As a thread of toffee is formed continue bringing spoons together and pulling apart until the toffee starts to set and threads are formed. Repeat to use all the toffee.

Croquembouche

Coconut Fluff Cake

Serves 12
Oven temperature 350°F, 180°C

³/₄ cup/90 g flour

¹/₄ cup/30 g cornstarch

1 cup/220 g superfine sugar

10 egg whites

¹/₂ teaspoon salt

1 teaspoon cream of tartar

2 tablespoons water

1 teaspoon vanilla

1 cup/45 g shredded dry coconut

FLUFFY FROSTING
¹/₂ cup/125 mL water

1¹/₄ cups/315 g sugar

3 egg whites

**1³/₄ cups/90 g shredded dry coconut,
lightly toasted**

1　Sift together flour and cornstarch three times, then sift once more with ¹/₄ cup/60 g of the superfine sugar.

2　Place egg whites, salt, cream of tartar and water in a large bowl and beat until stiff peaks form. Do not overbeat or the egg whites will break and lose structure. Beat in vanilla, then fold in remaining sugar, 1 tablespoon at a time.

3　Sift flour mixture over egg white mixture and gently fold in. Sprinkle coconut over top of batter and fold in. Spoon batter into a 10 in/25 cm ungreased tube pan, then draw a spatula gently through the mixture to break up any large air pockets. Bake for 45 minutes. When cake is cooked invert pan and allow cake to hang while it is cooling.

4　To make frosting, place water and sugar in a saucepan and cook over a medium heat, without boiling, stirring constantly, until sugar dissolves. Brush any sugar from sides of pan using a pastry brush dipped in water. Bring the syrup to the boil and boil rapidly for 3-5 minutes, without stirring, or until syrup reaches the soft-ball stage (239°F/115°C on a candy thermometer). Place egg whites in a bowl and beat until soft peaks form. Continue beating while pouring in syrup in a thin stream. Continue beating until all the syrup is used and frosting stands in stiff peaks. Spread frosting over top and sides of cold cake and press toasted coconut onto sides of cake.

Coconut Fluff Cake

Special Occasion Cakes 97

Hazelnut Cream Meringue

Serves 8
Oven temperature 300°F, 150°C

6 egg whites

1 cup/220 g superfine sugar

2 tablespoons cornstarch

3¹/₂ oz/100 g hazelnuts (filberts), ground

CHOCOLATE FILLING
1¹/₄ cups/315 mL whipping cream

2 tablespoons cocoa powder

2 tablespoons confectioners' sugar

CHOCOLATE HAZELNUT SAUCE
³/₄ cup/185 mL whipping cream

3 oz/90 g semi-sweet cooking chocolate, grated

6 tablespoons bottled chocolate hazelnut spread

1 Place egg whites in a large bowl and beat until soft peaks form. Gradually add sugar, beating well after each addition. Continue beating until mixture is thick and glossy.

2 Fold cornstarch and hazelnuts (filberts) into egg white mixture. Spread evenly over the base of two greased and lined 9 in/23 cm round layer pans and bake for 45 minutes. Allow meringues to stand in pans for 10 minutes before turning onto wire racks to cool.

3 To make filling, place cream, cocoa powder and confectioners' sugar in a bowl and beat until soft peaks form. Spread one meringue with filling, top with other meringue and dust with confectioners' sugar.

4 To make sauce, place cream, chocolate and chocolate hazelnut spread in a small saucepan and cook over a low heat, stirring constantly, until ingredients are combined. Remove pan from heat and set aside to cool slightly. Serve sauce with meringue.

Chocolate Rum Cake

Makes two 9 in/23 cm round layers
Oven temperature 350°F, 180°C

¹/₂ cup/1 stick/125 g butter or shortening

2 cups/350 g packed brown sugar

2 eggs, separated

1 cup/170 g golden seedless raisins, chopped

4 oz/125 g semi-sweet cooking chocolate, melted and cooled

2¹/₂ cups/315 g self-rising flour

¹/₂ teaspoon ground cinnamon

¹/₄ cup/60 mL hot water

¹/₂ cup/125 g dairy sour cream

COFFEE CREAM
1 tablespoon instant coffee powder

2 tablespoons boiling water

1 cup/2 sticks/250 g unsalted (sweet) butter, cut into pieces

4 cups/625 g confectioners' sugar

¹/₂ teaspoon vanilla

TO DECORATE
toasted sliced almonds

grated chocolate

1 Place butter or shortening and 1¹/₂ cups/250 g of the brown sugar in a bowl and beat until light and fluffy. Beat in egg yolks, remaining brown sugar, raisins and melted chocolate.

2 Sift flour, soda and cinnamon together. Add flour mixture, hot water and sour cream to butter mixture and mix well.

3 Place egg whites in a large bowl and beat until soft peaks form. Fold egg white mixture into batter. Spoon batter into two greased and lined 9 in/23 cm round layer pans and bake for 40 minutes or until cooked when tested with skewer. Sprinkle rum over hot cakes. Allow cakes to stand in pans for 10 minutes before turning onto wire racks to cool.

4 To make Coffee Cream, dissolve coffee powder in boiling water. Set aside to cool. Place butter in a bowl and beat until light and creamy. Add confectioners' sugar, coffee mixture and vanilla and continue beating until light and fluffy.

5 To assemble, cut each cake in half. Place one half on a serving plate, spread with Coffee Cream and top with a second cake half. Repeat layers ending with a layer of cake. Spread remaining Coffee Cream over top and sides of cake. Press almonds around sides of cake. Top with grated chocolate.

TRIPLE CHOCOLATE TERRINE

1 To make cake, place butter and vanilla in a bowl and beat until light and fluffy. Gradually add sugar, beating well, until mixture is creamy. Beat in eggs one at a time. Fold sifted flour and milk, alternately, into butter mixture. Spoon batter into a greased and parchment paper-lined 4½ x 8½ in/11 x 21 cm loaf pan and bake for 20-25 minutes or until cooked when tested with a skewer. Stand in pan for 5 minutes before turning onto a wire rack to cool.

2 To make fudge filling, place butter and confectioners' sugar in a bowl and beat until light and creamy. Fold in chocolate then cream. Refrigerate until required.

3 To make mousse, place chocolate and butter in a saucepan and cook over a low heat, stirring constantly, until well blended. Remove pan from heat and set aside to cool. Place eggs and sugar in a bowl and beat until thick and creamy. Fold chocolate mixture, cream, rum and gelatin mixture into egg mixture.

4 To assemble terrine, cut cake horizontally into three layers. Spread two layers with fudge filling and place one of these layers filling side upwards in the bottom of a 4½ x 8½ in/11 x 21 cm loaf pan lined with plastic wrap. Top with half the mousse and refrigerate for 10 minutes or until almost set. Place the second layer of filling-topped cake over the mousse with filling facing upwards. Top with remaining mousse and refrigerate until almost set. Place remaining cake layer on top and refrigerate until set.

5 To make glaze, place white chocolate and butter in a small saucepan and cook over a low heat, stirring constantly, until well blended. Set aside to cool slightly. Turn terrine onto a wire rack, trim edges, pour glaze over to cover and allow to set.

Serves 10
Oven temperature 350°F, 180°C

BUTTER CAKE
½ cup/1 stick/125 g butter

1 teaspoon vanilla

½ cup/100 g superfine sugar

2 eggs

1 cup/125 g flour, sifted
with 1 teaspoon baking powder

⅓ cup/90 mL milk

DARK CHOCOLATE FUDGE FILLING
½ cup/1 stick/125 g butter

2 tablespoons confectioners' sugar

3 oz/90 g semi-sweet cooking
chocolate, melted and cooled

1 cup/250 mL whipping cream, chilled

MILK CHOCOLATE MOUSSE
6½ oz/200 g milk chocolate, broken
into pieces

½ cup/1 stick/125 g unsalted (sweet)
butter

2 eggs

2 tablespoons superfine sugar

1 cup/250 mL whipping cream

1 tablespoon dark rum

2 tablespoons unflavored gelatin dissolved
in 2 tablespoons hot water, cooled

WHITE CHOCOLATE GLAZE
8 oz/250 g white chocolate, broken into
pieces

3 oz/90 g unsalted (sweet) butter

SOMETHING
HEALTHY

*Great tastes that are full
of goodness. Enjoy these cakes,
cookies and bars anytime of day for
snacks or treats. The recipes in this
chapter keep well and most will stand
up to life in a lunch box making
them ideal for packed lunches for
school and office.*

*Pineapple and Granola Cookies (page 102), Apricot
Date Bars (page 102), Winter Squash and Apricot Loaf (page 103)*

PINEAPPLE AND GRANOLA COOKIES

Makes 30
Oven temperature 350°F, 180°C

8 oz/250 g toasted granola

1 cup/125 g self-rising flour, sifted

1/2 cup/125 g granulated brown (raw or demerara) sugar

3 tablespoons/45 g chopped candied pineapple

1/2 cup/1 stick/125 g butter, melted

1 egg, lightly beaten

1　Place granola, flour, sugar and pineapple in a bowl. Add butter and egg and mix well to combine.

2　Place spoonfuls of mixture on greased baking sheets and bake for 12-15 minutes or until golden brown. Stand cookies on sheets for 5 minutes before transferring to wire racks to cool.

APRICOT DATE BARS

Makes 30
Oven temperature 375°F, 190°C

2/3 cup/90 g dried apricots, chopped

boiling water

2 cups/250 g flour, sifted
with 1/2 teaspoon baking soda

1 cup/170 g packed brown sugar

3/4 cup/75 g grated dry coconut

1/3 cup/60 g pitted dates, chopped

3/4 cup/1 1/2 sticks/185 g butter, melted

LEMON GLAZE
1/3 cup/90 g butter, softened

1 1/2 cups/220 g confectioners' sugar, sifted

2 tablespoons lemon juice

2 tablespoons/15 g grated dry coconut, toasted

1　Place apricots in a small bowl and pour over enough boiling water to cover. Set aside to soak for 10 minutes. Drain.

2　Sift flour and sugar together into a large bowl. Add coconut, dates and apricots, pour in melted butter and mix to combine. Press mixture into a shallow, greased and lined 7 x 11 in/18 x 28 cm cake pan and bake for 25 minutes or until firm. Allow to cool in pan.

3　To make glaze, place butter in a bowl and beat until light and creamy. Add confectioners' sugar and lemon juice and beat to make a glaze with an easy-to-spread consistency. Add a little more lemon juice if necessary. Spread glaze over cold layer and sprinkle with toasted coconut. Cut into bars.

WINTER SQUASH AND APRICOT LOAF

1 Place butter, sugar and vanilla in a large bowl and beat until light and creamy. Add eggs one at a time, beating well after each addition. Sift flour, baking soda, nutmeg and cinnamon together. Mix flour mixture and squash, alternately, into butter mixture. Fold in apricots.

2 Spoon batter into a greased and floured 4^1/$_2$ x 8^1/$_2$ in/ 11 x 21 cm/loaf pan and bake for 1 hour or until cooked when tested with a skewer. Stand in pan for 5 minutes before turning onto a wire rack to cool.

Makes a 4^1/$_2$ x 8^1/$_2$ in/11 x 21 cm loaf
Oven temperature 350°F, 180°C

^{3}/$_4$ cup/1^1/$_2$ sticks/185 g butter, softened

1 cup/170 g packed brown sugar

1 teaspoon vanilla

2 eggs

1^1/$_2$ cups/185 g flour, sifted

^{1}/$_8$ teaspoon baking soda

1 teaspoon ground nutmeg

^{1}/$_2$ teaspoon ground cinnamon

10 oz/315 g butternut or Hubbard squash, cooked and mashed

1 cup/125 g dried apricots, chopped

SWEET CORN AND CHEESE MUFFINS

1 Sift flour, baking powder and salt together in a bowl. Mix in sweet corn, Cheddar cheese and Parmesan cheese. Make a well in the center of the dry ingredients.

2 Place egg, milk and butter in a small bowl and whisk to combine. Pour milk mixture into dry ingredients and mix with a fork until ingredients are just combined. Take care not to overmix, the mixture should be coarse and lumpy.

3 Spoon batter into greased muffins cups and bake for 25 minutes or until muffins are well risen and golden brown. Turn muffins onto a wire rack to cool.

Makes 12
Oven temperature 350°F, 180°C

2 cups/250 g flour

1 tablespoon baking powder

^{1}/$_2$ teaspoon salt

10 oz/315 g canned sweet corn kernels, drained

^{1}/$_2$ cup/60 g Cheddar cheese, shredded

2 tablespoons grated Parmesan cheese

1 egg, lightly beaten

^{3}/$_4$ cup/185 mL milk

3 tablespoons/45 g butter, melted

HONEY OAT LOAF

Makes a 4¹/₂ x 8¹/₂ in/11 x 21 cm loaf
Oven temperature 350°F, 180°C

1¹/₂ cups/185 g flour

4 teaspoons baking powder

1 teaspoon salt

1 cup/90 g rolled oats

3 tablespoons/45 g butter, melted

2 eggs, lightly beaten

¹/₄ cup/60 mL water

¹/₂ cup/170 g honey, warmed

1 Sift flour, baking powder and salt together into a large bowl. Stir in rolled oats.

2 Combine butter, eggs, water and honey in a small bowl. Add egg mixture to flour mixture and mix until just combined. Pour batter into a greased and floured 4¹/₂ x 8¹/₂ in/ 11 x 21 cm loaf pan and bake for 40-45 minutes or until cooked when tested with a skewer. Stand loaf in pan for 5 minutes before turning onto a wire rack to cool.

Above: Honey Oat Loaf
Right: Fruity Cookies (page 106), Almond Fruit Bread

ALMOND FRUIT BREAD

1 Place egg whites and almond extract in a bowl and beat until soft peaks form. Add superfine sugar, a spoonful at a time, beating well after each addition.

2 Fold flour, almonds, cherries, pineapple, apricots and ginger into egg white mixture. Spoon mixture onto a lightly greased and lined 3½ x 10 in/8 x 25 cm loaf pan and bake for 35-40 minutes or until firm.

3 Turn loaf onto a wire rack to cool. Wrap loaf in aluminum foil and set aside for 1-2 days. Using a very sharp serrated knife, cut loaf into wafer thin slices. Place slices on a baking sheet lined with parchment paper and bake at 300°F/150°C for 35 minutes or until dry and crisp. Place on wire rack to cool.

Makes 30 slices
Oven temperature 350°F, 180°C

3 egg whites

1 teaspoon almond extract

¹/₂ cup/100 g superfine sugar

1 cup/125 g flour, sifted

¹/₂ cup/60 g slivered almonds

²/₃ cup/125 g candied cherries, chopped

¹/₃ cup/60 g candied pineapple, chopped

¹/₃ cup/60 g candied apricots, chopped

¹/₃ cup/60 g crystallized ginger, chopped

FRUITY COOKIES

Makes 16
Oven temperature 350°F, 180°C

¹/₄ cup/¹/₂ stick/60 g butter

¹/₃ cup/60 g packed brown sugar

2 tablespoons flour, sifted

1 teaspoon pumpkin pie spice

²/₃ cup/60 g pecans, finely chopped

1 tablespoon finely chopped candied cherries

1 tablespoon currants

1 tablespoon chopped mixed candied citrus peel

1 Place butter in a bowl and beat until light and fluffy. Gradually add sugar and beat until just combined.

2 Stir in flour, pie spice, pecans, cherries, currants and mixed peel. Place spoonfuls of mixture on lightly greased baking sheets, leaving 2 in/5 cm between each spoonful and bake for 15 minutes or until golden. Remove sheet from oven and, using a spatula, push cookies into a round shape. Stand on sheets for 1-2 minutes before transferring to wire racks to cool.

WHOLEWHEAT DATE BISCUITS

Makes 15
Oven temperature 425°F, 220°C

1 cup/125 g flour

1 cup/155 g wholewheat flour

4 teaspoons baking powder

1 cup/45 g unprocessed bran

¹/₄ cup/¹/₂ stick/60 g butter

³/₄ cup/125 g pitted dates, finely chopped

1 cup/125 mL milk

1 Sift flour, wholewheat flour and baking powder together into a bowl. Return grits to bowl. Add bran and mix to combine. Cut in butter until mixture resembles coarse bread crumbs. Add dates and mix to combine.

2 Make a well in the center of the dry ingredients and stir in enough milk to make a soft, sticky dough.

3 Turn dough onto a lightly floured surface and knead lightly until smooth. Press dough out to ¹/₂ in/1 cm thick and using a 2 in/5 cm biscuit cutter, cut out rounds.

4 Arrange biscuits close together on a greased and lightly floured baking sheet, brush with a little milk and bake for 15 minutes or until golden. Serve warm with butter, cream cheese or honey.

ALMOND AND APRICOT LOAF

1 Place apricots, butter or shortening, sugar and water in a bowl and mix until butter melts and sugar dissolves. Set aside to cool to room temperature. Stir in beaten egg.

2 Sift together flour, wholewheat flour and baking soda. Return grits to bowl. Fold flour mixture into apricot mixture. Stir in almonds.

3 Spoon batter into a greased and floured 4½ x 8½ in/ 11 x 21 cm loaf pan and bake for 1 hour or until cooked when tested with a skewer.

Makes a 4½ x 8½ in/11 x 21 cm loaf
Oven temperature 350°F, 180°C

⅔ cup/90 g dried apricots, chopped

¼ cup/½ stick/60 g butter or shortening

¾ cup/185 g sugar

1 cup/250 mL boiling water

1 egg, lightly beaten

1 cup/125 g flour

1 cup/155 g wholewheat flour

1 teaspoon baking soda

⅓ cup/60 g blanched almonds, chopped

YOGURT DATE LOAF

1 Place dates and apple juice in a small saucepan and bring to the boil over a medium heat. Remove pan from heat and set aside to cool completely.

2 Place yogurt, egg white and milk in a bowl and mix to combine. Sift flour, soda and pie spice together, then fold in date mixture.

3 Spoon batter into a greased and floured 4½ x 8½ in/ 11 x 21 cm loaf pan. Bake for 30 minutes or until cooked when tested with skewer. Stand in pan for 10 minutes before turning onto a wire rack to cool.

Makes a 4½ x 8½ in/11 x 21 cm loaf
Oven temperature 350°F, 180°C

½ cup/90 g pitted dates, chopped

½ cup/125 mL apple juice

½ cup/100 g plain yogurt

1 egg white

¼ cup/60 mL milk

2 cups/300 g wholewheat flour

½ teaspoon baking soda

½ teaspoon pumpkin pie spice

NO-CHOLESTEROL FRUIT CAKE

Makes a deep 9 in/23 cm round cake
Oven temperature 300°F, 150°C

³/₄ cup/60 g rice bran

1 kg/2 lb diced mixed dried and candied fruits and peels

³/₄ cup/125 g packed brown sugar

1 tablespoon finely grated orange rind

¹/₃ cup/90 mL orange juice

¹/₂ cup/125 mL stout or beer

³/₄ cup/185 mL hot water

¹/₃ cup/90 g polyunsaturated margarine, melted

2 cups/315 g wholewheat flour

¹/₂ teaspoon baking soda

¹/₂ teaspoon ground cinnamon

¹/₂ teaspoon ground ginger

¹/₂ teaspoon ground nutmeg

¹/₂ teaspoon ground cardamom

1 Place rice bran, dried fruit, sugar, orange rind, orange juice, ¹/₃ cup/90 mL of the stout or beer and water in a bowl and mix to combine. Set aside to cool slightly. Cover and stand at room temperature overnight.

2 Stir margarine, flour, soda, cinnamon, ginger, nutmeg and cardamom into fruit mixture and mix to combine. Spoon batter into a 3 in/7.5 cm deep, greased and lined 9 in/ 23 cm round cake pan or springform pan and bake for 1¹/₂ hours or until cooked when tested with a skewer. Remove cake from oven and pour over remaining stout or beer. Wrap cake in pan in aluminum foil and set aside to cool. When cold, turn cake out of pan and store in an airtight container.

Below: No-Cholesterol Fruit Cake
Right: Eggless Chocolate Cake, Quick Wholewheat and Fruit Rolls (page 110)

EGGLESS CHOCOLATE CAKE

1   Sift flour, cocoa powder and baking soda together into a bowl. Add sugar and mix to combine. Place molasses, butter, buttermilk and milk in a bowl and mix to combine. Stir milk mixture into dry ingredients and mix well to combine.

2   Spoon batter into a greased and floured 7 in/18 cm round cake pan and bake for 30 minutes or until cooked when tested with skewer. Allow cake to stand in pan for 10 minutes before turning onto a wire rack to cool.

3   To make frosting, place butter and milk in a bowl and mix to combine. Mix in cocoa powder and confectioners' sugar and beat for 5 minutes or until light and fluffy. Spread top and sides of cold cake with frosting.

Makes a 7 in/18 cm round cake
Oven temperature 350°F, 180°C

1¹/₂ cups/185 g flour

4 teaspoons cocoa powder

³/₄ teaspoon baking soda

³/₄ cup/185 g sugar

1 tablespoon light molasses

¹/₃ cup/90 g butter, melted

¹/₂ cup/125 mL buttermilk, warmed

¹/₂ cup/125 mL milk, warmed

CHOCOLATE FROSTING
¹/₄ cup/¹/₂ stick/60 g butter, softened

3-4 tablespoons milk

2 tablespoons cocoa powder, sifted

3 cups/470 g confectioners' sugar, sifted

QUICK WHOLEWHEAT AND FRUIT ROLLS

Makes 8
Oven temperature 400°F, 200°C

2 cups/315 g wholewheat flour

2 cups/250 g flour

³/₄ teaspoon baking soda

¹/₂ teaspoon ground nutmeg

¹/₂ teaspoon ground cinnamon

1 cup/155 g diced mixed dried and candied fruits and peels

1¹/₂ cups/375 mL buttermilk or soured milk

1 Sift wholewheat flour, white flour, baking soda, nutmeg and cinnamon together into a bowl. Return grits to bowl. Add dried fruit and mix to combine.

2 Stir buttermilk a little at a time into flour mixture and beat until dough is firm and leaves the sides of the bowl.

3 Turn dough onto a lightly floured surface and knead briefly. Divide dough into eight portions and shape into rolls. Place rolls on a lightly greased baking sheet and bake for 30-35 minutes or until well-risen and golden. Serve warm.

BANANA AND PINEAPPLE MUFFINS

Makes 12
Oven temperature 400°F, 200°C

1¹/₄ cups/200 g wholewheat flour

2 teaspoons baking powder

1 teaspoon pumpkin pie spice

¹/₃ cup/60 g packed brown sugar

1 cup/45 g oat bran

1 small banana, mashed

5 oz/155 g canned crushed pineapple, drained

3 egg whites, lightly beaten

2 tablespoons vegetable oil

¹/₂ cup/125 mL pineapple juice

1 Sift flour, baking powder and pie spice together into a bowl. Add sugar and bran and mix to combine.

2 Place banana, pineapple, egg whites, oil and juice in a bowl and mix to combine. Make a well in the center of the dry ingredients, add banana mixture and mix to combine.

3 Spoon batter into lightly greased muffin cups and bake for 12-15 minutes or until golden. Turn muffins onto a wire rack to cool. Serve warm.

APRICOT OAT BARS

1   Place butter or shortening and sugar in a bowl and beat until light and creamy. Beat in flour and baking soda. Stir in oats.

2   Press half the mixture into the base of a shallow, greased and lined 7 x 11 in/18 x 28 cm cake pan. Spread with jam, then sprinkle over remaining mixture and bake for 30 minutes or until firm. Cool layer in pan before turning out and cutting into triangles.

Makes 24
Oven temperature 350°F, 180°C

$\frac{1}{2}$ **cup plus 2 tablespoons/155 g butter or shortening**

1$\frac{1}{4}$ cups/220 g packed brown sugar

1$\frac{3}{4}$ cups/220 g flour, sifted

$\frac{1}{2}$ **teaspoon baking soda**

1$\frac{1}{2}$ cups/140 g rolled oats

$\frac{3}{4}$ **cup/230 g apricot jam**

SPICY APPLE CAKE

1   Place oil and sugar in a large bowl and mix to combine. Beat in eggs and vanilla.

2   Sift flour and pie spice together into a bowl. Place apples, lemon rind and raisins in a separate bowl and mix to combine. Fold flour mixture and apple mixture, alternately, into egg mixture.

3   Spoon batter into a greased 8 in/20 cm ring cake pan and bake for 30-35 minutes or until cooked when tested with a skewer. Stand in pan for 5 minutes before turning onto a wire rack to cool.

Cook's tip: Recipe can be baked in a greased and floured 8 in/20 cm springform pan, or 9 in/23 cm square pan, if desired.

Makes an 8 in/20 cm ring cake
Oven temperature 350°F, 180°C

$\frac{1}{4}$ **cup/60 mL vegetable oil**

$\frac{3}{4}$ **cup/170 g superfine sugar**

2 eggs, lightly beaten

1 teaspoon vanilla

1 cup/125 g self-rising flour

1$\frac{1}{2}$ teaspoons pumpkin pie spice

14 oz/440 g canned unsweetened sliced apples, drained

1 teaspoon finely grated lemon rind

$\frac{1}{2}$ **cup/90 g golden seedless raisins**

CHEESY APPLE MUFFINS

Makes 12
Oven temperature 400°F, 200°C

1¼ cups/200 g wholewheat flour

¼ teaspoon ground cinnamon

¼ teaspoon ground nutmeg

¼ teaspoon ground ginger

¼ teaspoon ground cloves

1 teaspoon baking powder

½ teaspoon baking soda

1 cup/45 g oat bran

¼ cup/45 g packed brown sugar

1 green apple, cored, peeled and shredded

4 oz/125 g ricotta cheese

2 tablespoons vegetable oil

¾ cup/185 mL apple juice

1 Sift flour, cinnamon, nutmeg, ginger, cloves, baking powder and soda together into a bowl. Add oat bran and sugar and mix to combine.

2 Make a well in the center of the flour mixture. Add apple, ricotta cheese, oil and apple juice and mix until just combined. Spoon batter into lightly greased muffin cups and bake for 25 minutes or until golden. Turn muffins onto a wire rack to cool.

Above: Banana and Pineapple Muffins (page 110), Cheesy Apple Muffins
Right: Fresh Herb and Oat Biscuits

Fresh Herb and Oat Biscuits

1 Place flour, oats and baking powder in a bowl and mix to combine. Cut in butter until mixture resembles fine bread crumbs. Stir in parsley, basil and rosemary.

2 Make a well in the center of the mixture and pour in milk. Mix lightly with a knife until all ingredients are just combined. Turn dough onto a lightly floured surface and knead briefly.

3 Pat dough out evenly to ³/₄ in/2 cm thick. Using a 2 in/5 cm biscuit cutter, cut out rounds. Arrange biscuits side by side in a lightly greased 8 in/20 cm round layer pan. Brush tops with a little milk and bake for 15-20 minutes or until biscuits are golden. Serve warm.

Makes 9
Oven temperature 425°F, 220°C

1¹/₂ cups/185 g flour, sifted
¹/₂ cup/45 g instant rolled oats
2 teaspoons baking powder
2 tablespoons/30 g butter
2 teaspoons chopped fresh parsley
2 teaspoons chopped fresh basil
2 teaspoons chopped fresh rosemary
³/₄ cup/185 mL milk

BRAN AND PEANUT COOKIES

Makes 45
Oven temperature 350°F, 180°C

4 cups/185 g bran flakes cereal, crumbled

2 cups/250 g flour, sifted

¹/₂ cup/90 g packed brown sugar

¹/₂ cup/75 g unsalted roasted peanuts

¹/₂ cup/125 g smooth peanut butter

¹/₂ cup/170 g honey, warmed

³/₄ cup/1¹/₂ sticks/185 g butter, melted

2 eggs, lightly beaten

1 Place bran flakes, flour, sugar and peanuts in a large bowl and mix to combine. Place peanut butter, honey, butter and eggs in a separate bowl and mix to combine. Add peanut butter mixture to bran mixture and mix well.

2 Place spoonfuls of mixture 1 in/2.5 cm apart on greased baking sheets. Bake for 10-12 minutes or until lightly browned. Allow cookies to cool on baking sheets.

CARROT CAKE

Makes a deep 8 in/20 cm square cake
Oven temperature 350°F, 180°C

2 cups/375 g ground rice (rice flour), sifted

2 teaspoons pumpkin pie spice

2 teaspoons baking soda

1 cup/170 g packed brown sugar

¹/₂ cup/1 stick/125 g butter or shortening, softened

4 small carrots, shredded

1¹/₄ cups/125 g pecans, chopped

1 cup/170 g golden seedless raisins

2 cups/400 g plain yogurt

1 teaspoon vanilla

confectioners' sugar

1 Place ground rice (rice flour), pie spice, baking soda, brown sugar, butter or shortening, carrots, pecans, raisins, yogurt and vanilla in a large bowl and mix well.

2 Spoon batter into a 3 in/7.5 cm deep, greased and lined 8 in/20 cm square cake pan and bake for 45-50 minutes or until cooked when tested with a skewer. Stand in pan for 10 minutes before turning onto a wire rack to cool. Dust with confectioners' sugar.

Cook's tip: Recipe can be baked in a greased and floured 8 in/20 cm fluted tube pan or 2 in/5 cm deep, 11 x 7 in/28 x 18 cm cake pan.

LEMON AND CARAWAY SEED CAKE

1 Place butter or shortening, sugar and lemon curd in a bowl and beat until light and creamy. Add eggs one at a time, beating well and adding ¹/₃ cup/45 g of the sifted flour after each egg. Stir in caraway seeds.

2 Spoon batter into a greased and floured 7 in/18 cm round cake pan and bake for 1 hour or until cooked when tested with a skewer. Stand in pan for 10 minutes before turning onto a wire rack to cool.

Cook's tip: Recipe can be baked in a 4-5 cup/1-1.25 liter greased and floured ring mold, if desired.

Makes a 7 in/18 cm round cake
Oven temperature 325°F, 160°C

³/₄ cup/1¹/₂ sticks/185 g butter or shortening

¹/₂ cup/100 g superfine sugar

7 tablespoons lemon curd

3 eggs

1 cup/125 g flour sifted
with ¹/₂ teaspoon baking soda

1 teaspoon caraway seeds

APPLE AND APRICOT LOAF

1 Place apricots, dried apples and orange juice in a small saucepan and bring to the boil over a medium heat. Remove pan from heat and set aside to cool to room temperature.

2 Add shredded apple, carrot, cocoa powder, pie spice, egg whites, flour and baking powder and mix well.

3 Spoon batter into a greased and floured 4¹/₂ x 8¹/₂ in/11 x 21 cm loaf pan and bake for 1 hour or until cooked when tested with a skewer. Stand in pan for 5 minutes before turning onto a wire rack to cool.

Makes a 4¹/₂ x 8¹/₂ in/11 x 21 cm loaf
Oven temperature 350°F, 180°C

1³/₄ cups/250 g dried apricots, chopped

2 cups/125 g dried apples, chopped

1¹/₄ cups/315 mL orange juice

1 apple, cored, peeled and shredded

1 small carrot, shredded

1 tablespoon cocoa powder

1 teaspoon pumpkin pie spice

2 egg whites, lightly beaten

1¹/₂ cups/230 g wholewheat flour

1¹/₂ teaspoons baking powder

BRAN DATE LOAF

Makes a 4½ x 8½ in/11 x 21 cm loaf
Oven temperature 375°F, 190°C

2 cups/250 g flour

¼ teaspoon ground cinnamon

¼ teaspoon ground nutmeg

1¼ teaspoons baking soda

¼ cup/45 g sugar

¼ cup/½ stick/60 g butter or shortening

1 cup/45 g unprocessed bran

1 egg, beaten

1 cup/250 mL milk

1¼ cups/185 g pitted dates, chopped

1   Place flour, cinnamon, nutmeg, baking soda and sugar in a food processor and process to sift. Add butter or shortening and bran and process for 1 minute longer.

2   Combine egg and milk. Stir egg mixture and dates into bran mixture. Spoon batter into a greased and floured 4½ x 8½ in/11 x 21 cm loaf pan and bake for 50-55 minutes or until cooked when tested with a skewer. Stand in pan for 5 minutes before turning onto a wire rack to cool.

Below: Bran and Peanut Cookies (page 114), Bran Date Loaf
Right: Carrot Cake (page 114), Fruity Rock Cakes

FRUITY ROCK CAKES

1 Sift together flour, baking soda and sugar in a mixing bowl. Cut in butter or shortening until mixture resembles fine bread crumbs. Stir in mixed fruit, lemon rind and orange rind. Add egg and milk and mix to form a soft dough.

2 Place tablespoons of mixture on greased baking sheets and dust lightly with cinnamon sugar mixture. Bake for 12-15 minutes or until golden. Remove from oven and transfer to wire racks to cool.

Makes 30
Oven temperature 350°F, 180°C

2 cups/250 g flour, sifted

¹/₂ teaspoon baking soda

¹/₄ cup/60 g superfine sugar

¹/₃ cup/90 g butter or shortening

³/₄ cup/125 g diced mixed dried and candied fruits and peels

1 teaspoon finely grated lemon rind

1 teaspoon finely grated orange rind

1 egg, lightly beaten

¹/₃ cup/90 mL milk

¹/₂ teaspoon cinnamon mixed with 2 tablespoons superfine sugar

Quick Banana Pecan Loaf

Makes a 4½ x 8½ in/11 x 21 cm loaf
Oven temperature 400°F, 200°C

1 cup/45 g unprocessed bran
1 cup/170 g packed brown sugar
3 small bananas, mashed
1 cup/250 mL milk
½ cup/60 g finely chopped pecans
1½ cups/185 g flour, sifted
1 teaspoon pumpkin pie spice
½ teaspoon baking soda

1　Place bran, sugar, bananas and milk in a bowl, mix to combine and set aside to stand for 5 minutes.

2　Add pecans, flour, pie spice and baking soda to banana mixture and mix well. Spoon batter into a greased and floured 4½ x 8½ in/11 x 21 cm loaf pan and bake for 1 hour or until cooked when tested with a skewer. Stand in pan for 5 minutes before turning onto a wire rack to cool.

Carrot and Sesame Muffins

Makes 24
Oven temperature 400°F, 200°C

3 cups/375 g self-rising flour
½ teaspoon baking soda
1 teaspoon pumpkin pie spice
½ cup/90 g packed brown sugar
1 large carrot, shredded
5 tablespoons toasted sesame seeds
1 cup/170 g golden seedless raisins
1 cup/200 g plain yogurt
1 cup/250 mL milk
¼ cup/60 mL melted butter
3 egg whites, lightly beaten

1　Sift flour, baking soda and pie spice together into a bowl. Add sugar, carrot, sesame seeds and raisins and mix well to combine.

2　Place yogurt, milk, butter and egg whites in a separate bowl and whisk to combine. Add yogurt mixture to flour mixture and mix until just combined. Spoon batter into lightly greased muffin cups and bake for 20 minutes or until golden. Turn muffins onto a wire rack to cool.

Cook's tip: If self-rising flour is unavailable, substitute with 3 cups all-purpose flour sifted with 1½ teaspoons cream of tartar and increase baking soda to 1¼ teaspoons.

Herb and Cheese Loaf

1 Sift wholewheat flour and baking soda into a bowl. Return grits to bowl. Stir in oats, bran, Cheddar cheese, Parmesan cheese, chives and parsley. Make a well in the center of the dry ingredients, add milk and oil and mix well.

2 Place egg whites in a bowl and beat until stiff peaks form. Fold egg white mixture into batter. Spoon batter into a greased and floured 4½ x 8½ in/11 x 21 cm loaf pan and bake for 40 minutes or until cooked when tested with a skewer. Stand in pan for 5 minutes before turning onto a wire rack to cool.

Makes a 4½ x 8½ in/11 x 21 cm loaf
Oven temperature 350°F, 180°C

1¼ cups/200 g wholewheat flour

½ teaspoon baking soda

1 cup/90 g rolled oats

1 cup/45 g unprocessed bran

½ cup/60 g shredded Cheddar cheese

1 tablespoon grated Parmesan cheese

2 tablespoons snipped fresh chives

2 tablespoons chopped fresh parsley

1 cup/250 mL milk

⅓ cup/90 mL vegetable oil

3 egg whites

Spiced Apple Wholewheat Cake

1 Place apples and water in a saucepan and cook over a medium heat until tender. Place apple mixture in a food processor or blender and process until smooth. Set aside to cool.

2 Place butter or shortening and sugar in a bowl and beat until light and fluffy. Add eggs one at a time, beating well after each addition.

3 Sift flour, wholewheat flour, baking soda and pie spice together into a bowl. Return grits to bowl. Mix flour mixture and apple mixture, alternately, into butter mixture, then stir in walnuts and raisins.

4 Spoon batter into a 3 in/7.5 cm deep, greased and lined 9 in/23 cm round cake pan or springform pan and bake for 40 minutes or until cooked when tested with a skewer. Stand in pan for 5 minutes before turning onto a wire rack to cool.

5 Split cake in half horizontally, spread bottom half with cream then top with other half and dust with confectioners' sugar.

Makes a deep 9 in/23 cm round cake
Oven temperature 350°F, 180°C

2 apples, cored, peeled and sliced

¾ cup/185 mL water

½ cup/1 stick/125 g butter or shortening

1 cup/250 g granulated brown (raw or demerara) sugar

2 eggs

1 cup/125 g flour

1 cup/155 g wholewheat flour

¾ teaspoon baking soda

1 teaspoon pumpkin pie spice

¼ cup/30 g walnuts, chopped

⅓ cup/60 g golden seedless raisins, chopped

¾ cup/185 mL whipping cream, whipped

confectioners' sugar, sifted

HONEY AND RICOTTA CARROT ROLL

Serves 8
Oven temperature 350°F, 180°C

4 eggs, separated

$^1/_2$ cup/100 g superfine sugar

$^1/_2$ cup/60 g flour

1 teaspoon ground cinnamon

1 teaspoon ground nutmeg

1 teaspoon ground allspice

1 large carrot, shredded

2 tablespoons honey

confectioners' sugar

APRICOT BRANDY FILLING
$^3/_4$ cup/100 g dried apricots, chopped

$^1/_2$ cup/125 mL brandy

8 oz/250 g ricotta or cottage cheese

$^1/_2$ cup/100 g plain yogurt

1 tablespoon honey

1 teaspoon ground nutmeg

2 tablespoons slivered almonds

1   Place egg yolks and sugar in a bowl and beat until pale and thick. Sift flour, cinnamon, nutmeg and allspice together into a bowl. Fold flour mixture and carrots, alternately, into egg yolk mixture.

2   Place egg whites in a separate bowl and beat until soft peaks form. Gradually add honey and continue beating until stiff peaks form. Fold egg white mixture into carrot mixture.

3   Spoon batter into a greased and lined 10$^1/_2$ x 12$^3/_4$ in/ 26 x 32 cm jelly roll pan and bake for 15-20 minutes or until firm to touch.

4   When roll is cooked, turn onto a sheet of parchment paper sprinkled with superfine sugar and roll up from the short end like a jelly roll. Set aside until cold.

5   To make filling, place apricots in a small bowl, pour over brandy and set aside to stand for at least 1 hour. Place ricotta or cottage cheese, yogurt, honey and nutmeg in a food processor or blender and process to combine. Drain apricots. Add apricots and almonds to cheese mixture and mix to combine.

6   Unroll cake and remove paper. Spread cake with filling and reroll. Sprinkle roll with sifted confectioners' sugar and cut into slices to serve.

Right: Honey and Ricotta Carrot Roll
Far right: Wholewheat Banana Cake

WHOLEWHEAT BANANA CAKE

1 Place bananas, walnuts, oil, raisins, oats, flour, baking powder and sugar in a bowl and mix well to combine.

2 Spoon batter into a greased and lined 8 in/20 cm round cake pan or springform pan and bake for 1 hour or until cooked when tested with a skewer. Stand in pan for 10 minutes before turning onto a wire rack to cool.

Makes a deep 8 in/20 cm round cake
Oven temperature 350°F, 180°C

3 large ripe bananas, mashed

¹/₃ cup/45 g chopped walnuts

³/₄ cup/185 mL vegetable oil

¹/₂ cup/100 g golden seedless raisins

³/₄ cup/75 g rolled oats

1 cup/155 g wholewheat flour, sifted and grits returned

2 teaspoons baking powder

¹/₄ cup/60 g sugar

Mocha Hazelnut Meringues

Makes 40
Oven temperature 250°F, 120°C

4 egg whites

1 teaspoon vanilla

$^1/_8$ teaspoon cream of tartar

$^1/_2$ cup/75 g confectioners' sugar

2 tablespoons cocoa powder

4 teaspoons instant coffee powder dissolved in 2 teaspoons boiling water

$5^1/_2$ oz/170 g hazelnuts (filberts), chopped and toasted

1 Place egg whites in a bowl and beat until soft peaks form. Add vanilla and cream of tartar and continue beating, while gradually adding sugar and cocoa powder. Continue beating until stiff peaks form. Add coffee mixture and beat well to combine. Fold hazelnuts (filberts) into mixture.

2 Drop heaped teaspoons of mixture onto baking sheets lined with parchment paper and bake for 1 hour. Turn oven off and leave meringues in oven for 5 minutes longer. Cool meringues on wire racks.

Pear Bread

Makes a $4^1/_2$ x $8^1/_2$ in/11 x 21 cm loaf
Oven temperature 350°F, 180°C

3 cups/375 g flour, sifted

1 teaspoon baking powder

$^3/_4$ teaspoon baking soda

$^1/_2$ teaspoon salt

$^1/_2$ cup/100 g superfine sugar

1 cup/155 g dried pears, soaked overnight, drained and chopped

2 tablespoons coarsely chopped pistachio nuts

1 teaspoon finely grated lemon rind

2 eggs

$^3/_4$ cup/185 mL milk

$^1/_4$ cup/60 mL melted butter, cooled

1 Place flour, baking powder, baking soda, salt, sugar, pears, pistachio nuts and lemon rind in a bowl and mix well to combine.

2 Place eggs and milk in a separate bowl and whisk to combine. Add egg mixture and melted butter to flour mixture and mix well.

3 Spoon batter into a greased and floured $4^1/_2$ x $8^1/_2$ in/ 11 x 21 cm loaf pan and bake for $1^1/_4$ hours or until cooked when tested with a skewer. Stand in pan for 5 minutes before turning onto a wire rack to cool.

DUTCH SPICE CAKE

1 Place butter or shortening and sugar in a bowl and beat until light and fluffy. Add eggs and milk and beat well.

2 Sift flour, salt, baking soda, cinnamon, cloves and nutmeg together into a bowl. Add flour mixture to butter mixture and mix well.

3 Spoon batter into a 3 in/7.5 cm deep, greased and lined 8 in/20 cm round cake pan or springform pan and bake for 1 hour or until cooked when tested with a skewer. Stand in pan for 5 minutes before turning onto a wire rack to cool.

Makes a deep 8 in/20 cm round cake
Oven temperature 350°F, 180°C

1/2 cup/1 stick/125 g butter or shortening

1 1/2 cups/265 g packed brown sugar

4 eggs, beaten

1/2 cup/125 mL milk

2 1/2 cups/315 g flour

1 teaspoon salt

1 1/2 teaspoons baking soda

2 teaspoons ground cinnamon

1/4 teaspoon ground cloves

1/4 teaspoon ground nutmeg

PUMPKIN AND PRUNE BREAD

1 Place white flour, wholewheat flour, baking powder, pie spice, baking soda and bran in a bowl and mix to combine. Place oil, egg, pumpkin, orange rind, prunes, orange juice and evaporated milk in a separate bowl and mix to combine.

2 Make a well in the center of the flour mixture, pour in squash mixture and mix lightly until ingredients are just combined.

3 Turn dough onto a lightly floured surface and knead briefly. Place dough on a greased baking sheet and shape into a 3/4 in/2 cm thick circle. Brush with a little milk and with a sharp knife mark into eight wedges. Bake for 45 minutes or until golden. Serve warm.

Serves 8
Oven temperature 400°F, 200°C

3 cups/375 g flour, sifted

1 cup/155 g wholewheat flour, sifted

4 teaspoons baking powder

2 teaspoons pumpkin pie spice

1/4 teaspoon baking soda

1/2 cup/20 g unprocessed bran

1/4 cup/60 mL vegetable oil

1 egg, lightly beaten

1 1/4 cups/315 g cooked mashed or canned pumpkin

1 tablespoon finely grated orange rind

1/2 cup/90 g chopped pitted prunes

1/2 cup/125 mL orange juice

1/2 cup/125 mL evaporated milk

SAVORY
TREATS

Cheese straws, quick breads and
pancakes are favorite savory baked
products and you will find them all in this
tasty chapter. Many of the recipes in this
section make great accompaniments for
soups and some, such as Pizza Bread,
when served with a salad make
a great weekend lunch.

Bacon and Leek Mini Quiches (page 126),
Bacon Corn Bread Pots (page 126), Cheese Straws (page 127)

BACON AND LEEK MINI QUICHES

Makes 20
Oven temperature 375°F, 190°C

favorite pastry for a 2-crust pie
BACON AND LEEK FILLING
2 slices bacon, finely chopped

1 small leek, finely chopped

1 tomato, finely chopped

1 tablespoon finely chopped fresh basil

freshly ground black pepper

4 eggs, lightly beaten

1¹/₂ cups/375 mL light cream (half-and-half)

¹/₂ cup/60 g shredded Cheddar cheese

1   To make filling, place bacon and leek in a nonstick skillet and cook over a medium heat for 3-4 minutes, or until leek is soft. Remove pan from heat and stir in tomato, basil and black pepper to taste. Set aside to cool. Place eggs and cream in a bowl and whisk to combine.

2   Roll out pastry to ¹/₈ in/3 mm thick. Cut out twenty pastry rounds using a 4 in/10 cm cutter and press lightly into greased flat-based tartlet pans.

3   Place a little bacon mixture into each pastry shell, spoon over egg mixture and sprinkle with cheese. Bake for 15-20 minutes or until filling is firm and pastry golden. Serve hot, warm or cold.

BACON CORN BREAD POTS

Makes 3 medium flowerpot loaves
Oven temperature 400°F, 200°C

4 slices bacon, finely chopped

1¹/₂ cups/250 g fine corn meal

1 cup/125 g flour

2¹/₂ teaspoons baking powder

4 teaspoons sugar

¹/₂ teaspoon salt

¹/₂ cup/60 g grated Parmesan cheese

¹/₃ cup/90 g butter, chopped

2 eggs, lightly beaten

1¹/₄ cups/315 mL buttermilk or soured milk

1   Place bacon in a nonstick skillet and cook over a medium heat for 3-4 minutes or until crisp. Remove bacon from pan and drain on paper towels.

2   Place corn meal, flour, baking powder, sugar, salt, Parmesan cheese and butter in a food processor and process until mixture resembles fine bread crumbs.

3   Combine eggs and milk and, with machine running, pour into corn meal mixture and process until just combined and batter is smooth. Take care not to overmix. Stir in bacon.

4   Spoon batter into three medium terracotta flowerpots lined with well-greased aluminum foil. Place on a baking sheet and bake for 25-30 minutes or until golden.

Cook's tip: The size of the flowerpots you use will affect the number of loaves you produce.

CHEESE STRAWS

1 If necessary, roll out pastry to $^1/_8$ in/3 mm thick. Combine Cheddar cheese, Parmesan cheese and paprika and sprinkle over one sheet of the pastry. Place remaining pastry sheet over cheese mixture, then roll together firmly, using a rolling pin.

2 Cut pastry square in half, then crosswise into strips $^1/_2$ in/1 cm wide and twist. Place on wet baking sheets and bake for 10 minutes or until puffed and golden. Remove from oven and transfer to wire racks to cool.

Makes 36-40
Oven temperature 400°F, 200°C

2 sheets prerolled frozen puff pastry, thawed

$^1/_2$ cup/60 g shredded Cheddar cheese

$^1/_2$ cup/60 g grated Parmesan cheese

1 teaspoon paprika

PANCAKE STACKS

1 Place flour, sugar, baking powder and salt in a food processor or blender. Combine egg, milk and butter and, with machine running, pour into flour mixture and process until smooth.

2 Cook spoonfuls of mixture in a greased skillet, over a medium-high heat, until bubbles form on the surface. Turn and cook until golden brown. Serve warm and stacked with the filling of your choice.

Asparagus and Chicken Pancakes: This is a delectable and different savory filling for pancakes. Melt 1 tablespoon/ 15 g butter in a small saucepan, stir in 1 tablespoon flour and cook over a medium heat for 1 minute. Remove pan from heat and gradually blend in $^1/_2$ cup/125 mL milk and $^1/_2$ cup/125 mL chicken stock. Return pan to heat and cook, stirring constantly, until sauce boils and mixture thickens. Stir in 1 cup/250 g chopped cooked chicken, $^1/_2$ cup/125 g chopped and blanched asparagus spears, $^1/_2$ teaspoon paprika and freshly ground black pepper to taste. Serve pancakes with chicken mixture.

Sweet serving suggestions: Pancakes are delicious topped with any of the following: sugar and freshly squeezed lemon juice; honey and butter; vanilla ice cream, chocolate fudge sauce and toasted nuts . . . and, of course, maple syrup!

Serves 4

1 cup/125 g flour

1$^1/_2$ tablespoons superfine sugar

1$^3/_4$ teaspoons baking powder

$^1/_2$ teaspoon salt

1 egg, lightly beaten

$^3/_4$ cup/185 mL milk

$^1/_4$ cup/$^1/_2$ stick/60 g butter, melted

PIZZA BREAD

Serves 4
Oven temperature 375°F, 190°C

1½ cups/185 g flour

½ cup/60 g rye or wholewheat flour

1 teaspoon baking powder

1 teaspoon baking soda

⅓ cup/90 g butter or shortening, melted

¾-1 cup/185-250 mL buttermilk

¼ cup/60 mL tomato paste

2 tablespoons chopped fresh oregano
or 2 teaspoons dried oregano

freshly ground black pepper

3 oz/90 g salami, thinly sliced

1 onion, thinly sliced

1 tomato, thinly sliced

4 tablespoons grated Parmesan cheese

3 tablespoons pine nuts (pignola)

6 oz/185 g mozzarella cheese, shredded

1 Sift flour, rye or wholewheat flour, baking powder and baking soda together into a mixing bowl. Mix in butter or shortening and enough buttermilk to form a soft dough.

2 Turn onto a floured surface and knead lightly until smooth. Press into a greased 10½ x 12¾ in/26 x 32 cm in jelly roll pan.

3 Spread dough with tomato paste, sprinkle with oregano and black pepper to taste, then top with salami, onion, tomato, Parmesan cheese, pine nuts (pignola) and mozzarella cheese. Bake for 15-20 minutes or until topping is golden and base is cooked through.

Pancake Stacks (page 127), Pizza Bread

CHEESY WHOLEWHEAT PARATHAS

1 Place flour and wholewheat flour in a food processor and process to sift. Add ¼ cup/60 g of the butter or shortening and process until mixture resembles coarse bread crumbs.

2 With machine running, add water and process to form a dough. Turn dough onto a lightly floured surface and knead for 5 minutes or until smooth. Set aside to stand for 5 minutes.

3 Place mashed potato, cheese, curry powder and cumin in a bowl and mix to combine.

4 Divide dough into twelve equal portions and press out each portion to form a 4 in/10 cm circle. Divide potato mixture between dough circles and spread evenly over dough, leaving a border around the edge. Fold dough circles in half to enclose the filling, then carefully roll again to form a 4 in/10 cm circle.

5 Melt remaining butter in a large skillet or griddle and cook a few parathas at a time for 3-4 minutes each side or until golden and cooked through. Serve warm.

Serving suggestion: Parathas are an unleavened Indian bread. This version with its cumin-flavored potato and cheese filling is delicious served with meat and vegetable curries.

Makes 12

3 cups/375 g flour

1 cup/155 g wholewheat flour

½ cup/1 stick/125 g plus 2 tablespoons/30 g butter or shortening

1½ cups/375 mL water

8 oz/250 g mashed potato

1 cup/125 g shredded Cheddar cheese

2 teaspoons curry powder

1 teaspoon ground cumin

CHILI SOUP BISCUITS

1 Place bacon in a nonstick skillet and cook over a medium-high heat for 3-4 minutes or until crisp. Remove from pan and drain on paper towels.

2 Sift flour, baking powder and salt together into a bowl. Cut in butter until mixture resembles coarse bread crumbs.

3 Stir bacon, cheese and chilies into flour mixture. Add milk and mix to form a soft dough. Turn onto a floured surface and knead lightly with fingertips until smooth.

4 Using heel of hand, gently press dough out to ½ in/1 cm thick. Cut out rounds using a 2 in/5 cm biscuit cutter and place on a greased baking sheet. Brush with melted butter and bake for 12-15 minutes or until golden brown. Transfer to wire racks to cool or serve warm spread with butter.

Makes 16 biscuits
Oven temperature 425°F, 220°C

2 slices bacon, finely chopped

2 cups/250 g flour

1 tablespoon baking powder

½ teaspoon salt

⅓ cup/90 g butter or shortening

¾ cup/90 g shredded Cheddar cheese

2 small red chilies, seeded and finely chopped

⅔ cup/170 mL milk

2 tablespoons/30 g butter, melted

MINI ASPARAGUS AND CHEESE CROISSANTS

Makes 12
Oven temperature 425°F, 220°C

1 sheet prerolled frozen puff pastry, thawed

1 egg, lightly beaten with 1 tablespoon water

ASPARAGUS AND CHEESE FILLING
4 stalks asparagus, blanched and finely chopped

$1/_2$ cup/60 g shredded Gruyère cheese

$1/_4$ teaspoon paprika

freshly ground black pepper

1 To make filling, place asparagus, cheese, paprika and black pepper to taste in a bowl and mix to combine.

2 Roll out pastry sheet to $1/_8$ in/3 mm thick (about 12 in/30 cm square) and cut into 4 in/10 cm wide strips. Cut each strip into triangles with 4 in/10 cm bases.

3 Place a little filling across the base of each triangle, roll up from the base and mold into a croissant shape. Brush with egg mixture.

4 Place croissants on greased baking sheets and bake for 12-15 minutes or until puffed and golden. Serve hot or cold.

Ham and Cheese Croissants: Melt 1 tablespoon/15 g butter in a skillet, add $1/_2$ cup/100 g finely chopped ham and 2 finely chopped spring onions and cook over a medium heat for 3-4 minutes or until onions are soft. Remove from heat, stir in 2 teaspoons finely chopped parsley and season to taste with black pepper. Set filling aside to cool. Add $1/_3$ cup/45 g shredded Cheddar cheese. Assemble and cook as for Mini Asparagus and Cheese Croissants.

Chocolate Croissants: As a filling for these delicious morsels use $1^1/_2$ oz/45 g grated milk or semi-sweet cooking chocolate. Place a little chocolate across the base of each triangle, roll up from the base and mold into a croissant shape. Brush with egg mixture and cook as for Mini Asparagus and Cheese Croissants.

CHIVE AND CHEESE SAVORIES

Makes 30
Oven temperature 350°F, 180°C

1 cup/125 g flour, sifted

$1/_4$ teaspoon baking soda

$1/_2$ cup/1 stick/125 g butter or shortening

2 oz/60 g blue cheese, crumbled

2 tablespoons grated Parmesan cheese

3 tablespoons snipped fresh chives

4 tablespoons sesame seeds

1 Place flour, baking soda, butter or shortening, blue cheese, Parmesan cheese and chives in a food processor and process until ingredients cling together. Turn onto a lightly floured surface and knead briefly. Wrap dough in plastic wrap and refrigerate for 30 minutes.

2 Roll teaspoonfuls of mixture into balls, then roll in sesame seeds. Place on lightly greased baking sheets, press with a fork and bake for 10 minutes. Remove from oven and transfer to wire racks to cool. Serve warm with soups or as part of an appetizer tray.

CHEESY SPINACH PIZZA

Serves 8
Oven temperature 400°F, 200°C

8 large spinach leaves, stalks removed and shredded

¹/₂ cup/20 g unprocessed bran

³/₄ cup/185 mL water

2 tablespoons olive oil

1³/₄ cups/215 g/7 oz self-rising flour

¹/₂ teaspoon baking powder

¹/₄ teaspoon baking soda

pinch ground nutmeg

freshly ground black pepper

TOPPING

¹/₃ cup/90 mL tomato paste

1 tablespoon finely chopped fresh basil

1 cup/125 g shredded mozzarella cheese

4 spring onions, finely chopped

2 tomatoes, sliced

¹/₄ cup/30 g grated Parmesan cheese

1   Steam or microwave spinach until tender. Drain and set aside to cool.

2   Place bran and water in a mixing bowl. Stand for 10 minutes, then stir in oil. Sift together flour, baking powder, soda and nutmeg. Stir into bran mixture with black pepper to taste and one-third of the cooked spinach.

3   Turn mixture out onto a lightly floured board and knead lightly. Press dough into lightly greased 12 in/30 cm metal pizza pan.

4   To make topping, combine tomato paste and basil and spread over pizza base. Top with mozzarella cheese, remaining spinach and spring onions. Arrange tomato slices on top, sprinkle with Parmesan cheese and bake for 30-35 minutes or until cooked and golden. Serve hot, warm or cold.

PESTO PINWHEELS

Makes 10
Oven temperature 425°F, 220°C

2 cups/250 g flour

1 teaspoon baking powder

¹/₂ teaspoon baking soda

2 teaspoons sugar

3 tablespoons/45 g butter or shortening

1 egg, lightly beaten

³/₄ cup/185 mL milk

¹/₂ cup/60 g shredded Cheddar cheese

PESTO FILLING

3 oz/90 g fresh basil leaves

3 cloves garlic, crushed

3 tablespoons pine nuts (pignola), toasted

¹/₄ cup/60 mL olive oil

¹/₄ cup/30 g grated Parmesan cheese

freshly ground black pepper

1   To make filling, place basil, garlic, pine nuts (pignola) and 2 tablespoons oil in food processor or blender and process until smooth. With machine running, gradually add remaining oil. Transfer to a small bowl and mix in Parmesan cheese and black pepper to taste.

2   Sift flour, baking powder and soda together into a bowl, then mix in sugar. Cut in butter or shortening, until mixture resembles fine bread crumbs. Make a well in the center of the flour mixture and mix in egg and ¹/₂ cup/125 mL of the milk to make a soft dough, adding a little more milk if necessary.

3   Turn dough onto a lightly floured surface and knead with fingertips until smooth. Roll out dough to form a rectangle ¹/₂ in/1 cm thick. Spread with filling and roll up like a jelly roll. Cut into ³/₄ in/2 cm slices and place on a lightly greased and floured baking sheet. Brush with remaining milk and sprinkle with Cheddar cheese. Bake for 15-20 minutes or until pinwheels are cooked. Serve warm.

MINI OLIVE QUICHES

Makes 4
Oven temperature 400°F, 200°C

1 sheet prerolled frozen puff pastry, thawed

¹/₂ cup/125 mL milk

3 eggs, lightly beaten

¹/₃ cup/90 mL whipping cream

¹/₄ cup/30 g shredded Cheddar cheese

1 teaspoon ground paprika

freshly ground black pepper

10 stuffed green olives, sliced

1 Line four 3 in/7.5 cm tartlet pans with pastry. Line each pastry shell with parchment paper, fill with uncooked rice and bake for 5 minutes. Remove rice and paper and bake for 5 minutes longer.

2 Place milk, eggs, cream, cheese, paprika and black pepper to taste in a bowl and mix to combine.

3 Divide olives between pastry shells, then pour over egg mixture. Reduce oven temperature to 350°F/180°C and bake for 15-20 minutes or until quiches are set. Serve hot, warm or cold.

Cook's tip: Individual quiches are great to keep in the freezer to have on hand for snacks and lunch boxes. One of these quiches when frozen will take about 10 minutes to heat in an oven preheated to 400°F/200°C.

MIXED HERB MUFFINS

Makes 12
Oven temperature 375°F, 190°C

2 cups/250 g flour, sifted

2 tablespoons sugar

1 tablespoon baking powder

1 egg

¹/₂ cup/125 mL milk

2 tablespoons/30 g butter, melted

2 oz/60 g chopped mixed fresh herbs, such as parsley, thyme, oregano and sage

1 Sift flour, sugar and baking powder together into a mixing bowl. Make a well in the center of the flour mixture and add egg, milk and butter. Mix to combine, then stir in herbs.

2 Spoon batter into lightly greased muffin cups and bake for 15-20 minutes or until muffins are cooked. Turn muffins onto a wire rack to cool.

PIZZAS, BREADS
AND BISCUITS

*Bread has been the 'staff of life'
for over 8000 years. You will never
tire of the feeling of satisfaction when
you lift a loaf of golden-brown bread
from the oven. In this chapter you will
see how easy it is to bake a variety of
wonderful breads and pizzas.*

*Wholewheat Cottage Loaf (page 136),
Hazelnut Bread (page 137), Wholewheat Rolls (page 136),
Herb Onion Loaves (page 138), White Bread (page 137)*

WHOLEWHEAT COTTAGE LOAF

Makes 1 loaf
Oven temperature 400°F, 200°C

1 teaspoon brown sugar

1³/₄ cups/440 mL warm water (110-115°F/ 51-52°C)

1 package active dry yeast

2 cups/250 g flour, sifted

2 cups/315 g wholewheat flour, sifted and grits returned

1 teaspoon salt

1 tablespoon superfine sugar

1 tablespoon/15 g butter

1 egg, lightly beaten

1 tablespoon sesame seeds

1   Dissolve brown sugar in water, then sprinkle yeast over and set aside in a warm place for 10 minutes or until mixture is frothy.

2   Place flour, wholewheat flour, salt and superfine sugar in a bowl and mix to combine. Cut in butter and make a well in the center, then pour in yeast mixture. Mix to form a soft dough. Turn dough onto a lightly floured surface and knead for 5-8 minutes or until dough is smooth and elastic.

3   Place dough in a lightly greased bowl, cover with plastic wrap and set aside to stand in a warm place for 30 minutes or until doubled in size.

4   Punch down and turn dough onto a lightly floured surface. Knead for 5 minutes or until smooth. Divide dough into two making one portion twice the size of the other. Shape both portions of dough into round balls. Place the large ball onto a lightly greased baking sheet and flatten slightly. Using your index and second fingers make an indentation in the center of the ball. Dampen the top of the larger ball with a little water and place the smaller ball on it. To secure, push your index and second fingers through the top of the base. Brush with egg and sprinkle with sesame seeds. Cover with plastic wrap and set aside in a warm place for 30 minutes or until dough is doubled in size.

5   Bake for 30-40 minutes or until the base of the loaf sounds hollow when tapped with fingers. Serve warm or transfer to a wire rack to cool.

Wholewheat Rolls: Shape dough into a long sausage shape, then cut into even-sized pieces. Roll each piece of dough to form a small ball. Brush rolls with egg and sprinkle with sesame seeds. Place on greased baking sheets, cover with plastic wrap and set aside to rise. Bake for 20-25 minutes or until cooked. This quantity of dough will make 10 rolls.

HAZELNUT BREAD

Makes 2 loaves
Oven temperature 400°F, 200°C

1 package active dry yeast

¼ cup/60 mL warm water (110-115°F/ 51-52°C)

3 cups/375 g flour, sifted

1 cup/125 g rye flour, sifted

2 teaspoons salt

2 eggs, lightly beaten

¾ cup/185 mL extra warm water

4 oz/125 g hazelnuts (filberts), coarsely chopped and toasted

EGG GLAZE

1 egg yolk, lightly beaten

1 tablespoon water

pinch salt

1 Sprinkle yeast over warm water and stir to dissolve. Place flour, rye flour and salt in a bowl and mix to combine. Make a well in center of dry ingredients. Stir in yeast mixture, eggs and sufficient water to make a soft dough. Turn dough onto a lightly floured surface and knead for 5-8 minutes or until smooth and elastic. Place dough in a large, greased bowl, cover with plastic wrap and set aside in a warm place until doubled in size.

2 Punch down and turn dough onto a lightly floured surface. Knead in hazelnuts (filberts). Divide dough in half, mold each half into an oval shape and place on a greased baking sheet. Cover loosely and set aside in a warm place until doubled in size.

3 To make glaze, whisk together egg yolk, water and salt. Brush each loaf with glaze and bake for 30-35 minutes or until golden. Cool on wire racks.

WHITE BREAD

Makes 1 large loaf
Oven temperature 350°F, 180°C

2 tablespoons sugar

1⅓ cups/330 mL milk, warmed (110-115°F/51-52°C)

1 package active dry yeast

4 cups/500 g flour, sifted

2 teaspoons salt

2 tablespoons/30 g butter

1 egg yolk, lightly beaten

2 tablespoons sesame or poppy seeds

1 Dissolve 2 teaspoons of the sugar in milk, then sprinkle over yeast and set aside in a warm place for 10 minutes or until frothy.

2 Place flour, salt and remaining sugar in a large mixing bowl. Cut in butter and make a well in the center, then pour in yeast mixture and egg yolk. Mix to form a soft dough. Turn onto a lightly floured surface and knead for 5-8 minutes, or until dough is smooth and elastic.

3 Place in a lightly greased bowl, cover with plastic wrap and set aside to stand in a warm place for 30 minutes or until dough is doubled in size.

4 Punch down and turn dough onto a lightly floured surface. Knead for 5 minutes or until smooth. Divide dough into two equal portions and roll each into a strip 4 in/10 cm wide and ½ in/1 cm thick. Roll up each strip from the short end and place rolls side by side (spiral end to spiral end) in a large, greased and floured bread pan. Cover with plastic wrap and set aside in a warm place for 30 minutes or until doubled in size. Brush loaf with a little milk and sprinkle with sesame seeds.

5 Bake for 50-55 minutes, or until base of loaf sounds hollow when tapped with fingers. Turn onto a wire rack to cool.

BISCUITS

Makes 12
Oven temperature 425°F, 220°C

2 cups/250 g flour

4 teaspoons baking powder

2 teaspoons sugar

1/2 teaspoon salt

1/2 cup/1 stick/125 g butter or shortening

2/3 cup/170 mL milk

1   Sift together flour, baking powder, sugar and salt. Cut in butter or shortening until mixture resembles coarse crumbs.

2   Make a well in the center of flour mixture and pour in milk. Mix to form a soft dough, then turn onto a lightly floured surface and knead briefly.

3   Pat or roll dough out to 1/2 in/1 cm thick. Cut out biscuits using a floured 2 in/5 cm round cutter. Avoid twisting the cutter or the biscuits will rise unevenly.

4   Arrange biscuits close together on a baking sheet or in an 8 in/20 cm round cake pan. Brush tops, if desired, with a little milk and bake for 12-15 minutes or until cooked and golden. Serve warm with butter or whipped cream and jam.

Cook's tip: For richer biscuits, substitute the 2/3 cup/170 mL milk with a mixture of 1 beaten egg and 1/2 cup/125 mL milk

HERB ONION LOAVES

Makes 2 loaves
Oven temperature 400°F, 200°C

1 1/2 oz (1 1/2 cakes)/45 g compressed yeast or 2 packages active dry yeast

1/4 cup/60 mL lukewarm water (110-115°F/ 51-52°C)

3 cups/375 g flour, sifted

3 cups/470 g wholewheat flour, sifted and grits returned

1 tablespoon sugar

2 teaspoons salt

2 tablespoons chopped mixed fresh herbs, such as parsley, chives, rosemary and thyme

2 tablespoons dried onion flakes

freshly ground black pepper

1/2 cup/1 stick/125 g butter, melted and cooled

1 egg, lightly beaten

2/3 cup/170 mL evaporated milk

1 cup/250 mL warm water

1 tablespoon corn meal

1   Dissolve yeast in lukewarm water. Set aside until frothy.

2   Place flour, wholewheat flour, sugar, salt, herbs, onion flakes and black pepper to taste in a large bowl and mix to combine. Combine butter, egg, milk and warm water. Make a well in the center of flour mixture. Pour in butter and yeast mixtures and mix to form a soft dough.

3   Turn dough onto a lightly floured surface and knead for 5-8 minutes or until dough is smooth and elastic. Divide dough into six equal portions and roll each into a long sausage, tapering slightly at ends. Braid three portions together to form a loaf. Repeat with remaining dough.

4   Cover a wire rack with a clean cloth and lightly dust with wholewheat flour. Place loaves on cloth, cover with plastic food wrap and stand in a warm place for 30 minutes or until doubled in size.

5   Lift loaves carefully onto hot baking sheets lightly dusted with corn meal and bake for 30-35 minutes or until golden and base sounds hollow when tapped with fingers.

Variation: Divide dough in half, roll out one piece to an 8 x 12 in/20 x 30 cm rectangle. Roll up to make a long thin loaf. Make four or five slashes with a sharp knife across top of loaf. Repeat with remaining dough and bake as above.

Fruit and Spice Medallions

Makes 20

1 cup/125 g flour

1 teaspoon baking powder

1 teaspoon pumpkin pie spice

3 tablespoons superfine sugar

3 tablespoons chopped golden seedless raisins

1 egg, lightly beaten

1/2 cup/125 mL milk

1/3 cup/90 mL whipping cream

1 Sift flour, baking powder and pie spice together into a bowl. Stir in sugar and raisins.

2 Place egg, milk and cream in a small bowl and whisk to combine. Make a well in the center of the flour mixture, then gradually stir in milk mixture and mix until smooth.

3 Cook tablespoons of mixture in a heated, greased, heavy-based skillet or griddle for 2-3 minutes or until bubbles appear on the surface, then turn and cook for 2-3 minutes longer or until golden. Serve warm or cold.

Cook's tip: Serve these sweet and fruity mini pancakes spread with butter and honey or jam at children's birthday parties, special brunches or as a treat for a coffee break.

Quick Herb Rolls

Makes 12 rolls
Oven temperature 350°F, 180°C

1/3 cup/90 g butter

8 spring onions, finely chopped

3 1/2 cups/435 g flour

4 teaspoons baking powder

1/2 teaspoon baking soda

1 tablespoon sugar

1 tablespoon finely chopped fresh parsley

1 tablespoon finely chopped fresh basil

1/2 cup/125 mL buttermilk or soured milk

3 eggs, lightly beaten

1 egg, beaten with 1 1/2 teaspoons olive oil

1 Melt butter in a skillet, add spring onions and cook over a medium heat for 2-3 minutes or until onions are soft. Remove pan from heat and set aside.

2 Sift flour, baking powder and soda together into a large bowl. Stir in sugar, parsley and basil. Place buttermilk or soured milk, eggs and onion mixture in a separate bowl and mix to combine. Add milk mixture to flour mixture and mix to form a firm dough.

3 Turn dough onto a lightly floured surface and knead until smooth. Divide dough into twelve portions. Roll each portion into a ball then place on a greased and floured baking sheet. Brush each roll with egg and oil mixture and bake for 30-35 minutes or until rolls are cooked. Serve warm or cold.

PECAN FRUIT LOAF

Makes a 4¹/₂ x 8¹/₂ in/11 x 21 cm loaf
Oven temperature 350°F, 180°C

1¹/₂ cups/315 g diced mixed dried and candied fruits and peels

1 cup/250 mL water

¹/₂ cup/1 stick/125 g butter or shortening

1¹/₂ cups/375 g sugar

1 egg

2 cups/250 g flour

1¹/₂ teaspoons baking powder

¹/₄ teaspoon baking soda

1¹/₄ cups/125 g pecans, coarsely chopped

1 Place fruit and water in a large saucepan, bring to the boil and cook for 3 minutes. Remove pan from heat and set aside to cool.

2 Place butter or shortening and sugar in a bowl and beat until light and creamy. Add egg and continue to beat until well combined. Sift flour, baking powder and soda together. Mix flour mixture and undrained fruit mixture, alternately, into butter mixture. Fold in pecans.

3 Spoon batter into a greased and lined 4¹/₂ x 8¹/₂ in/11 x 21 cm loaf pan and bake for 1¹/₄ hours or until cooked when tested with skewer. Stand in pan for 5 minutes before turning onto a wire rack to cool.

SODA BREAD

Makes 1 loaf
Oven temperature 400°F, 200°C

4 cups/500 g flour

1 teaspoon baking soda

1 teaspoon salt

3 tablespoons/45 g butter or shortening

2 cups/500 mL buttermilk or soured milk

1 Sift flour, baking soda and salt together into a bowl. Cut in butter or shortening until mixture resembles coarse bread crumbs. Make a well in the center of the flour mixture and pour in buttermilk or soured milk. Mix to form a soft dough.

2 Turn dough onto a floured surface and knead lightly until smooth. Shape into a 7 in/18 cm round loaf and place on a greased and floured baking sheet. Score dough into eighths using a sharp knife. Dust lightly with flour and bake for 35-40 minutes or until loaf sounds hollow when tapped with fingers. Serve warm cut into wedges.

Serving suggestion: Soda Bread is wonderful spread with butter and honey or light molasses.

SPICY COCONUT APPLE TWISTS

Makes 2 loaves
Oven temperature 350°F, 180°C

2 cups/250 g flour, sifted

$\frac{1}{2}$ teaspoon salt

2 tablespoons sugar

$\frac{1}{4}$ teaspoon ground cloves

$\frac{3}{4}$ teaspoon ground cinnamon

$\frac{1}{2}$ oz ($\frac{1}{2}$ cake)/15 g compressed yeast
or $\frac{1}{2}$ package active dry yeast

$\frac{3}{4}$ cup/185 mL milk, warmed

3 tablespoons/45 g butter or shortening,
melted

$5\frac{1}{2}$ oz/170 g canned unsweetened
apple slices, drained

COCONUT GLAZE

$\frac{3}{4}$ cup/125 g confectioners' sugar

1 tablespoon/15 g butter

$\frac{1}{2}$ teaspoon vanilla

$\frac{1}{3}$ cup/30 g grated dry coconut

3-4 tablespoons hot water

1 Place flour, salt, sugar, cloves and $\frac{1}{2}$ teaspoon of the cinnamon in bowl and mix to combine. Dissolve yeast in milk and stand in a warm place for 10 minutes or until mixture is frothy. Add yeast mixture and butter or shortening to flour mixture and mix to form a soft dough. Turn onto a lightly floured surface and knead for 5-8 minutes or until dough is smooth and elastic. Place in a lightly greased bowl, cover with plastic wrap and set aside to stand for 10 minutes.

2 Divide dough into four portions and roll each into a 3 x 12 in/8 x 30 cm strip. Spoon apple down center of each strip and sprinkle with remaining cinnamon. Fold in half lengthwise and seal edges. Roll each into a sausage shape. Twist 2 rolls together and place on a greased baking sheet. Repeat with remaining rolls.

3 Cover with plastic wrap and set aside to stand in a warm place for 20 minutes or until doubled in size. Bake for 20-25 minutes or until golden and cooked.

4 To make glaze, place confectioners' sugar, butter, vanilla and coconut in a bowl. Mix in enough water to make a glaze with a thin consistency. Spread glaze over hot twists.

EASY BERRY BREAD

Makes a 7 in/18 cm round loaf
Oven temperature 425°F, 220°C

3 cups/375 g flour

1 teaspoon baking powder

$\frac{3}{4}$ teaspoon baking soda

$1\frac{1}{2}$ teaspoons pumpkin pie spice

2 tablespoons sugar

2 tablespoons/30 g butter

$\frac{1}{2}$ cup/125 mL milk

$\frac{2}{3}$ cup/170 mL water

$6\frac{1}{2}$ oz/200 g raspberries

1 tablespoon superfine sugar

1 Sift flour, baking powder, baking soda and pie spice together into a bowl. Add sugar and cut in butter until mixture resembles coarse bread crumbs.

2 Make a well in the center of flour mixture, add milk and water and mix to form a soft dough.

3 Turn dough onto a lightly floured surface and knead until smooth. Divide dough into two portions and flatten each into a 7 in/18 cm round. Sprinkle raspberries and superfine sugar over surface of one round leaving 1 in/2.5 cm around edge. Brush edge with a little milk and place remaining round on top. Seal edges securely using fingertips.

4 Place loaf on a greased and lightly floured baking sheet, brush surface with milk and bake for 10 minutes. Reduce oven temperature to 350°F/180°C and bake for 20-25 minutes longer or until cooked. Serve warm.

BASIC PIZZA DOUGH

Makes enough dough for a 15-16 in/
38-40 cm pizza

¹/₂ package active dry yeast or ¹/₂ oz
(¹/₂ cake)/15 g compressed yeast

pinch sugar

1¹/₃ cups/330 mL warm water (110-115°F/
51-52°C)

¹/₂ cup/125 mL olive oil

4 cups/500 g flour, sifted

1¹/₄ teaspoons salt

1   Place yeast, sugar and water in bowl and mix to dissolve yeast. Set aside in a warm place for 5 minutes or until frothy. Stir in oil, flour and salt and mix until a rough dough forms. Turn dough onto a lightly floured surface and knead for 5 minutes or until soft and satiny. Add more flour if necessary.

2   Lightly oil a large bowl then roll dough around it to cover surface with oil. Cover bowl with plastic wrap and place in a warm place for 1¹/₂-2 hours or until dough is doubled in size.

3   Punch down, turn onto a lightly floured surface and knead briefly. Roll dough out to desired shape. If dough feels too stiff, set aside to rest for a few minutes and repeat process.

4   Place dough on an oiled pizza pan and finish shaping by hand, forming a slightly raised rim. The dough should be approximately ¹/₄ in/5 mm thick. For a thicker crust, cover with a clean teatowel and set aside for 30 minutes to rise again. The pizza is now ready for topping and baking.

To make in a food processor: Place flour and salt in a food processor and pulse once or twice to sift. With machine running, slowly pour in yeast mixture and oil and process for 10-15 minutes longer. Turn dough onto a lightly floured surface and knead by hand for 3-4 minutes. Complete as for basic recipe.

QUICK PIZZA DOUGH

Makes enough dough for a 15-16 in/
38-40 cm pizza

4¹/₃ cups/540 g flour, sifted

2 tablespoons/45 g superfine sugar

1 teaspoon salt

2 eggs, lightly beaten

1 cup/250 mL olive oil

¹/₂ cup/125 mL white wine

1   Place flour, sugar and salt in a bowl and mix to combine. Gradually mix in eggs, oil and wine, beating well to combine.

2   When a loose dough forms, turn onto a lightly floured surface and knead for 2-3 minutes or until smooth and satiny. Use immediately or cover and refrigerate until required. Bring dough to room temperature before rolling out and using.

Cook's tip: If some of the oil separates during storage, knead the dough again to incorporate the oil before using.

1 Place yeast and sugar in a large bowl and stir in all but 1 tablespoon water. Cover and set aside in a warm place for 8-10 minutes or until frothy.

2 Stir oil and remaining water into yeast mixture. Add one-third of the flour and stir until smooth. Stir in half the remaining flour and beat, then add remaining flour. Mix until a soft dough forms. Turn dough onto a lightly floured surface and knead for 8-10 minutes or until dough is smooth and satiny.

3 Lightly oil a large bowl then roll dough around it to cover surface with oil. Cover bowl with plastic wrap and set aside in a warm place for 1½ hours or until dough is doubled in size.

4 Punch dough down, turn onto a lightly floured surface and knead briefly, then roll into desired shape. Place on an oiled baking sheet, brush surface with a little oil, cover with a clean teatowel and set aside to rise for 30 minutes longer.

5 Dimple the surface of the dough by pushing your fingertips about halfway into it. Traditionally this serves to create little pools for the olive oil, but it also kneads the dough one last time. Cover dough again with a clean teatowel and set aside in a warm place for 1½-2 hours or until dough is doubled in size. The focaccia is now ready for dressing and baking.

FOCACCIA DOUGH

Makes enough dough for an 11 x 15 in/ 28 x 38 cm focaccia or a 13 in/33 cm round

½ package active dry yeast

1 teaspoon sugar

1¼ cups/315 mL warm water (110-115°F/ 51-52°C)

1 tablespoon olive oil

4 cups/500 g flour, sifted

RICOTTA FOCACCIA

1 Prepare Focaccia Dough, as described in recipe through to the end of step 3. Punch down dough and knead briefly. Divide mixture into two portions and roll each out to make a thin 13 in/33 cm round.

2 Place one round on a greased pizza pan and spread evenly with ricotta cheese. Sprinkle with basil, cover with second round of dough and seal edges. Dimple surface with fingertips, brush with 1 tablespoon olive oil, cover with a clean teatowel and set aside in a warm place for 1-2 hours or until doubled in size.

3 Brush surface of focaccia with remaining olive oil, sprinkle with salt and bake for 20-25 minutes or until golden. Place focaccia on a wire rack to cool.

Makes a 13 in/33 cm round loaf
Oven temperature 400°F, 200°C

Ingredients for Focaccia Dough (see above)

8 oz/250 g ricotta cheese, well drained

1 tablespoon chopped fresh basil

¼ cup/60 mL olive oil

1 tablespoon coarse sea salt

CHEESE AND BACON PANZEROTTI

Makes 20-25
Oven temperature 350°F, 180°C

Ingredients for Quick Pizza Dough (see page 144)
CHEESE AND BACON FILLING
1 lb/500 g ricotta cheese, drained
6 oz/185 g smoked mozzarella cheese, finely diced
5 oz/155 g bacon slices, trimmed of fat, finely diced
1¹/₂ tablespoons grated Parmesan cheese
¹/₂ teaspoon freshly ground black pepper
3¹/₂ tablespoons fresh bread crumbs
2 tablespoons finely chopped fresh mint
3 eggs, lightly beaten

1   Prepare Quick Pizza Dough as described in recipe. Divide dough into two portions. Roll out each portion on a floured surface to ¹/₈ in/3 mm thick and using a 4 in/10 cm cutter, cut out rounds.

2   To make filling, place ricotta cheese, mozzarella cheese, bacon, Parmesan cheese, black pepper, bread crumbs, mint and half the egg mixture in a bowl and mix to combine.

3   Place a heaped tablespoon of mixture in the center of each dough round. Brush edges with some of the remaining egg mixture, then fold over to form a half circle or crescent. Using a fork, press edges together to seal and make a decorative pattern. Place panzerotti on greased baking sheets, brush surfaces with remaining egg mixture and bake for 12-15 minutes or until puffed and golden. Serve hot, warm or cold.

CHICKEN AND ASPARAGUS CALZONE

Makes 1 large calzone
Oven temperature 400°F, 200°C

¹/₂ ingredients for Basic Pizza Dough (see page 144)
1 large zucchini, sliced
salt
6 oz/185 g asparagus spears, trimmed, blanched and cut into 2 in/5 cm pieces
8 oz/250 g cooked chicken, cut into 1 in/2.5 cm pieces
1 oz/30 g ham, diced
4 oz/125 g ricotta cheese, drained
1 tablespoon grated Parmesan cheese
freshly ground black pepper
olive oil

1   Prepare Basic Pizza Dough as described in recipe.

2   Place zucchini in a sieve, sprinkle with salt and set aside to drain for 20 minutes. Rinse under cold running water and pat dry with paper towels.

3   Place zucchini, asparagus, chicken, ham, ricotta cheese, Parmesan cheese, black pepper to taste and a little olive oil in a bowl and mix to combine.

4   Roll out dough to a ¹/₄ in/5 mm thick, 12 in/30 cm round. Pile filling on one half of round, then fold uncovered side over filling. Fold edges up to seal, then crimp or flute to neaten.

5   Place calzone on an oiled baking sheet, brush with olive oil and bake for 20-25 minutes or until golden. Stand for 10 minutes before serving.

Ricotta Focaccia (page 145), Cheese and Bacon Panzerotti, Chicken and Asparagus Calzone

GRISSINI WITH FENNEL SEEDS

Makes 20-25 sticks
Oven temperature 400°F, 200°C

Ingredients for Basic Pizza Dough (see page 144)

4 tablespoons coarse sea salt

2 tablespoons fennel seeds

1   Prepare Basic Pizza Dough as described in recipe to end of step 2. Punch down, remove from bowl and knead briefly.

2   Cut dough into four equal portions. Shape each portion into a rectangle ½ in/1 cm thick. Sprinkle with salt and fennel seeds. Cut each piece of dough into 5-6 strips each about ½ in/1 cm wide.

3   Place strips 2 in/5 cm apart on lightly oiled baking sheets. Stretch slightly and bake for 15 minutes or until golden. Place grissini on wire racks to cool before storing in airtight containers.

ROSEMARY AND GARLIC WHOLEWHEAT SCHIACCIATA

Makes 3 schiacciata
Oven temperature 400°F, 200°C

Ingredients for Focaccia Dough (see page 145), substitute 1 cup/125 g flour with the same quantity of wholewheat flour

3-4 tablespoons olive oil

4 cloves garlic, crushed

2 tablespoons chopped fresh rosemary

1 tablespoon coarse sea salt

1   Prepare Focaccia Dough, as described in recipe, to the end of step 3.

2   Punch down dough, turn onto a lightly floured surface and knead briefly. Divide dough into three portions and shape into balls. Roll out each ball to form a circle ¼ in/5 mm thick. Place circles on oiled baking sheets, brush with a little olive oil and cover with clean teatowels. Set aside to rise in a warm place for 45 minutes or until puffy.

3   Place garlic and remaining olive oil in a small saucepan and heat over a low heat for 7-8 minutes. Remove pan from heat and set aside to cool for 30 minutes. Remove garlic and discard.

4   Using fingertips, dimple surface of bread. Brush with garlic-flavored olive oil and sprinkle with rosemary and salt. Bake for 20 minutes or until golden. Stand on sheets for 5 minutes before serving, or transfer to wire racks to cool.

OLIVE AND PANCETTA FOCACCIA

1 Make up Focaccia Dough as described in recipe to end of step 4.

2 Brush dough with oil, sprinkle with olives and pancetta and bake for 20-25 minutes or until golden. Serve warm or transfer to a wire rack to cool.

Makes 1 loaf
Oven temperature 400°F, 200°C

Ingredients for Focaccia Dough (see page 145)

3 tablespoons olive oil

4 oz/125 g black olives, sliced

4 oz/125 g pancetta or salt pork, diced

SPINACH, OLIVE AND ONION BREAD

1 Prepare Focaccia Dough, as described in recipe to end of step 3.

2 To make filling, heat olive oil in a large skillet, add onion and cook over a medium heat, stirring occasionally, for 4-5 minutes or until onion is soft. Add garlic and raisins and cook for 1 minute longer. Stir in spinach and olives and cook over a medium heat, stirring, for 5 minutes or until spinach begins to wilt. Remove pan from heat, add mozzarella cheese and black pepper to taste and mix to combine. Set aside.

3 Punch dough down, turn onto a lightly floured surface and knead briefly. Divide dough into four portions. Roll out each portion to form a round 1/4 in/5 mm thick. Place two rounds on oiled baking sheets, spread with filling to within 1 in/2.5 cm of edge. Cover with remaining rounds and pinch edges together to seal.

4 Brush top of each loaf with olive oil. Cover with a clean teatowel and set aside in a warm place for 45 minutes or until doubled in size.

5 Brush top of each loaf with egg white and bake for 25 minutes or until golden and well risen. Serve warm.

Makes 2 loaves
Oven temperature 400°F, 200°C

Ingredients for Focaccia Dough (see page 145)

1 tablespoon olive oil

1 egg white, lightly beaten

SPINACH FILLING
2 tablespoons olive oil

1 large red onion, sliced

1 clove garlic, crushed

1 tablespoon chopped golden seedless raisins

1 1/2 lb/750 g spinach, stalks removed, leaves shredded

4 oz/125 g stuffed green olives, sliced

3 tablespoons shredded mozzarella cheese

freshly ground black pepper

FRIED FLATBREAD

Makes 18

1 recipe Quick Pizza Dough (see page 144)

1 small red pepper, finely chopped

1 small onion, finely chopped

12 pitted olives, finely chopped

2 cloves garlic, crushed

vegetable oil for frying

1   Make up Quick Pizza Dough as described in recipe, adding red pepper, onion and olives to dry ingredients in step 1. Turn dough onto a lightly floured surface and knead. Set aside to rest for $1\frac{1}{2}$ hours.

2   Divide dough into 18 portions and using floured hands, roll each portion into a ball. Roll out each ball to form a $\frac{1}{8}$ in/3 mm thick round. Sprinkle one side of each round with garlic, then roll lightly.

3   Heat 1 tablespoon vegetable oil in a heavy-based skillet, add a bread round and cook until edges are golden and beginning to bubble. Turn once during cooking. Add more oil if necessary. Remove bread from pan, drain on paper towels and place on wire racks to cool. Repeat with remaining bread rounds.

Cook's tip: Cold flatbreads will keep in an airtight container for up to 1 week.

GARLIC FOCACCIA

1 Make up Focaccia Dough as described in recipe to end of step 4.

2 Combine oil and garlic and brush over dough. Sprinkle with salt and bake for 20-25 minutes or until golden. Serve warm or transfer to a wire rack to cool.

Makes 1 loaf
Oven temperature 400°F, 200°C

Ingredients for Focaccia Dough (see page 145)

3 tablespoons olive oil

4 cloves garlic, crushed

1 tablespoon coarse sea salt

From left: Grissini with Fennel Seeds (page 148), Rosemary and Garlic Wholewheat Schiacciata (page 148), Fried Flatbread, Garlic Focaccia, Spinach, Olive and Onion Bread (page 149)

GORGONZOLA AND SAGE PIZZA

Serves 6
Oven temperature 425°F, 220°C

1/2 ingredients for Basic Pizza Dough or Quick Pizza Dough (see page 144)

3/4 cup/185 mL olive oil

1 large eggplant, cut into 1/4 in/5 mm slices

155 g/5 oz Gorgonzola or soft blue cheese

12 oz/375 g ricotta cheese, drained

1 teaspoon finely chopped fresh sage or 1/4 teaspoon dried sage

3 tablespoons pine nuts (pignola)

3 tablespoons grated Parmesan cheese

freshly ground black pepper

fresh sage leaves (optional)

1 Prepare Basic Pizza Dough or Quick Pizza Dough as described in recipe. Shape dough into a 15 in/38 cm circle and place on a lightly greased pizza pan. Bring up sides to form a slight rim.

2 Heat 1/2 cup/125 mL oil in a large skillet and cook eggplant a few slices at a time until lightly browned on both sides. Remove from pan and drain on paper towels.

3 Place Gorgonzola or blue cheese and ricotta cheese in a bowl and mix well to combine. Spread cheese mixture evenly over dough. Top with eggplant slices, then sprinkle with sage, pine nuts (pignola), Parmesan cheese and black pepper to taste. Finally drizzle with remaining olive oil and top with fresh sage leaves, if using.

4 Bake for 15 minutes, then reduce oven temperature to 375°F/190°C and bake for 10 minutes longer. Serve hot or warm.

ARTICHOKE AND SALAMI PIZZA

Serves 6
Oven temperature 425°F, 220°C

1/2 ingredients for Basic Pizza Dough or Quick Pizza Dough (see page 144)

10 oz/315 g mozzarella cheese, thinly sliced

4 oz/125 g salami, thinly sliced

4 canned artichoke hearts, thinly sliced lengthwise

freshly ground black pepper

1 Prepare Basic Pizza Dough or Quick Pizza Dough as described in recipe. Roll out dough into a rectangle 1/2 in/1 cm thick and press into a lightly oiled, shallow 7 x 11 in/18 x 28 cm cake pan. Bring dough up at sides to form a slight rim. Brush with olive oil.

2 Place slices of mozzarella cheese, salami and artichoke hearts slightly overlapping in lines along width of dough to cover entire surface. Sprinkle generously with olive oil and season to taste with black pepper.

3 Bake for 15 minutes, then reduce oven temperature to 375°F/190°C and bake for 10 minutes longer or until cheese is bubbling and crust is golden. Remove from oven and stand briefly before serving.

1 Prepare Basic Pizza Dough as described in recipe. Brush a 13 in/33 cm metal pizza pan with olive oil and line with dough, pressing dough up sides to form a 1¹/₂ in/4 cm rim. Brush dough with oil and set aside.

2 To make sauce, heat oil in a large skillet, add onion, green pepper and garlic and cook over a medium heat, stirring, for 6-8 minutes or until onion is soft. Stir in tomatoes, sugar, chopped anchovy fillets and black pepper to taste.

3 To assemble, place tuna, lemon juice and black pepper to taste in a bowl and mix to combine. Reserve 2 olives for garnishing. Sprinkle one-third mozzarella cheese and 1 tablespoon Parmesan cheese over pizza dough. Top with half the tuna mixture, sprinkle with 1 tablespoon parsley and half the olives. Spoon half the sauce over, then repeat layers, finishing with a layer of mozzarella cheese and remaining Parmesan cheese.

4 Fold excess dough back on itself and crimp edges neatly. Arrange anchovy fillets in a diamond pattern on top of pizza. Halve remaining olives and place one in the center of each diamond. Drizzle with a little olive oil and bake for 15-20 minutes or until golden. Serve hot or warm.

DEEP-PAN TUNA PIZZA

Serves 6
Oven temperature 425°F, 220°C

Ingredients for Basic Pizza Dough (see page 144)

olive oil

14 oz/440 g canned tuna, drained, broken into chunks

lemon juice

freshly ground black pepper

2 oz/60 g pitted black olives

12 oz/375 g shredded mozzarella cheese

4 tablespoons grated Parmesan cheese

2 tablespoons chopped fresh parsley

10 whole anchovy fillets, drained and halved lengthwise

TOMATO SAUCE

2 tablespoons olive oil

1 large red onion, sliced lengthwise

1 green pepper, sliced

1 clove garlic, crushed

4 tomatoes, peeled, seeded and chopped

¹/₂ teaspoon sugar

1 tablespoon finely chopped anchovy fillets

PIES AND PASTRIES

Until the eighteenth century,
pies contained a mixture of sweet
and savory ingredients in a crust that was
merely a container to hold the filling.
Whether it is a picnic in the park, a
family dinner or a special occasion,
you are sure to find the perfect pie
for the occasion in this chapter.

Individual Meat Pies (page 157), High-Rise Apple Pie (page 157),
Bacon, Leek and Apple Tart (page 156)

PALMIERS

Makes 18
Oven temperature 425°F, 220°C

1 sheet prerolled frozen puff pastry, thawed

1 tablespoon/15 g butter, melted and cooled

3 tablespoons granulated brown (raw or demerara) sugar

1   Roll out pastry sheet to a 10 in/25 cm square.

2   Brush pastry with butter and sprinkle with a little sugar. Fold two opposite edges of pastry halfway towards the center. Sprinkle with a little more sugar and fold, taking edges to the center. Sprinkle with a little more sugar and fold one half of the pastry over the other half. Press lightly to join.

3   Cut pastry crosswise into eighteen slices and place on a greased baking sheet. Flatten slightly and bake for 10-15 minutes or until puffed and golden.

Pistachio Palmiers: Combine 1 tablespoon/15 g finely chopped unsalted pistachio nuts and 3 tablespoons packed brown sugar, and sprinkle over pastry in place of raw sugar.

Serving suggestion: Try sandwiching the Palmiers together with whipped cream. Delicious!

BACON, LEEK AND APPLE TART

Serves 8
Oven temperature 425°F, 220°C

PASTRY
2 cups/250 g flour, sifted

¹/₂ teaspoon salt

¹/₂ cup/125 g butter or shortening

4 tablespoons iced water

APPLE AND LEEK FILLING
1 tablespoon/15 g butter

1 cooking apple, cored, peeled and sliced

3 small leeks, washed, trimmed and sliced

4 slices bacon, chopped

¹/₄ teaspoon ground cloves

¹/₄ teaspoon ground nutmeg

2 oz/60 g blue vein cheese, crumbled

3 eggs, lightly beaten

³/₄ cup/185 mL whipping cream

2 tablespoons port

freshly ground black pepper

1   To make pastry, place flour and salt in a large bowl, cut in butter or shortening until mixture resembles coarse bread crumbs. Mix in enough water to form a firm dough. Turn dough onto a floured surface and knead lightly. Wrap pastry in plastic wrap and refrigerate for 30 minutes.

2   To make filling, melt butter in a skillet, add apple, leeks and bacon and cook over a medium heat, stirring, for 6-8 minutes or until apple is soft. Add cloves and nutmeg and cook for 1 minute longer. Remove pan from heat and set aside to cool.

3   Roll out pastry on a lightly floured surface and line the bottom and sides of a greased 9 in/23 cm tart pan with removable base. Prick bottom and sides of pastry with a fork and bake for 10 minutes.

4   Spread apple mixture over bottom of pastry shell. Place blue vein cheese, eggs, cream, port and black pepper to taste in bowl and mix to combine. Carefully pour egg mixture into pastry shell. Reduce oven temperature to 350°F/180°C and bake for 30-35 minutes or until firm. Serve hot, warm or cold.

INDIVIDUAL MEAT PIES

Makes 8 individual pies
Oven temperature 425°F, 220°C

favorite pastry for a 2-crust pie

1 sheet prerolled frozen puff pastry, thawed

1 egg, lightly beaten

BEEF FILLING

1¹/₂ lb/750 g very lean ground beef

2 cups/500 mL beef stock

freshly ground black pepper

8 teaspoons cornstarch blended with ¹/₂ cup/125 mL water

1 tablespoon Worcestershire sauce

1 teaspoon soy sauce

1 To make filling, heat a nonstick skillet, add beef and cook over a medium heat, stirring constantly, for 6-8 minutes or until beef browns. Drain pan of any juices and add stock. Season to taste with black pepper.

2 Bring beef mixture to the boil, then reduce heat, cover and simmer, stirring occasionally, for 20 minutes. Stir in cornstarch mixture, Worcestershire and soy sauces and cook, stirring constantly, until mixture boils and thickens. Remove pan from heat and set aside to cool.

3 Line bottom and sides of eight greased small metal pie pans or muffin cups with favorite pie pastry. Cut rounds of puff pastry to fit top of pies. Divide filling evenly between pie dishes. Brush edges of pastry with water and top with rounds of puff pastry. Press edges together to seal. Brush tops of pies with egg and bake for 5 minutes, then reduce oven temperature to 350°F/180°C and bake for 10-15 minutes longer or until tops of pies are golden and crisp.

HIGH-RISE APPLE PIE

Serves 8
Oven temperature 425°F, 220°C

PASTRY

3 cups/375 g flour, sifted

1 tablespoon confectioners' sugar, sifted

³/₄ cup/1¹/₂ sticks/185 g butter shortening, chilled

¹/₂ cup/125 mL iced water

1 egg white, lightly beaten

superfine sugar

APPLE FILLING

6 large cooking apples, cored, peeled and sliced

¹/₂ teaspoon ground cinnamon

2 tablespoons flour

4 tablespoons sugar

2 tablespoons/30 g butter, cut into small pieces

1 To make pastry, place flour and confectioners' sugar in a large mixing bowl mix to combine. Cut in butter or shortening until mixture resembles coarse bread crumbs. Mix in enough water to form a firm dough. Turn dough onto a lightly floured surface and knead lightly until smooth. Wrap pastry in plastic wrap and refrigerate for 30 minutes.

2 Roll out three-quarters of the pastry on a lightly floured surface and line the bottom and sides of a 2 in/5 cm deep, lightly greased 8 in/20 cm quiche dish or casserole. Trim edges with a sharp knife.

3 To make filling, place apple slices, cinnamon, flour and sugar in a bowl and mix to combine. Arrange apple mixture in pastry shell, shaping apples to a dome in the center. Dot with butter.

4 Roll out remaining pastry on a lightly floured surface, large enough to cover pie. Brush edge of pastry with water and cover with pastry top. Press edges together to seal, then trim and make a decorative edge using fingertips. Make two slits in top of pie to allow steam to escape. Brush with egg white, sprinkle with superfine sugar and bake for 20 minutes. Reduce oven temperature to 350°F/180°C and cook for 40-45 minutes longer, or until apples are tender when tested with skewer.

Lemon and Lime Meringue Pie

Serves 8
Oven temperature 400°F, 200°C

PASTRY
³/₄ cup/1¹/₂ sticks/185 g butter or shortening

4 tablespoons superfine sugar

1¹/₂ cups/185 g flour

²/₃ cup/75 g cornstarch

LEMON AND LIME FILLING
4 tablespoons flour, sifted

4 tablespoons cornstarch, sifted

1 teaspoon finely grated lemon rind

1 teaspoon finely grated lime rind

¹/₂ cup/125 mL lemon juice

¹/₄ cup/60 mL lime juice

1 cup/250 g sugar

1¹/₄ cups/315 mL water

¹/₃ cup/90 g butter, chopped

4 egg yolks, lightly beaten

MERINGUE TOPPING
4 egg whites

1 teaspoon vanilla

¹/₂ teaspoon cream of tartar

¹/₂ cup/100 g superfine sugar

1   To make pastry, place butter or shortening and superfine sugar in a large bowl and beat until light and creamy. Sift flour and cornstarch together and gradually mix into butter mixture. Turn dough onto a lightly floured surface and knead briefly. Press mixture over bottom and sides of a 2 in/5 cm deep, greased 9 in/23 cm quiche dish or casserole. Prick bottom and sides with a fork and bake for 20-25 minutes. Remove from oven and set aside to cool.

2   To make filling, place flour, cornstarch, lemon rind, lime rind, lemon juice, lime juice, sugar and water in a saucepan and blend until smooth. Cook over a medium heat, stirring constantly, for 3-4 minutes or until mixture boils and thickens. Reduce heat and cook, stirring constantly, for 3 minutes longer.

3   Remove pan from heat and add butter and egg yolks. Stir until butter melts, then set aside to cool completely. Pour filling into pastry shell and set aside.

4   To make topping, place egg whites, vanilla and cream of tartar in a large mixing bowl and beat until soft peaks form. Add sugar a little at a time, beating well after each addition. Continue to beat until mixture is glossy and stiff peaks form.

5   Spoon topping over filling, spreading out to pastry edge to seal. Bake at 350°F/180°C for 5-10 minutes or until lightly browned. Remove from oven and set aside to cool.

Right: Lemon and Lime Meringue Pie
Far right: Spicy Pumpkin Tart (page 160)

SHORTBREAD PASTRY

1½ cups/185 g flour

¼ cup/30 g/1 oz cornstarch

½ cup/1 stick/125 g butter, cut into cubes

⅓ cup/75 g superfine sugar

1 egg, lightly beaten

1 egg yolk, lightly beaten

1 teaspoon vanilla

1 Place flour, cornstarch, butter and sugar in a food processor or blender and process until mixture resembles coarse bread crumbs. Combine egg, egg yolk and vanilla and, with machine running, add to flour mixture, continuing to process until a soft dough forms.

2 Turn dough onto a floured surface and knead lightly. Wrap in plastic wrap and refrigerate for 30 minutes. Use as desired.

Cook's tip: You can expect this rich, crisp and tender pastry to be similar to a shortbread cookie in flavor and texture; an unusual alternative to traditional pastry for sweet pies.

SPICY PUMPKIN TART

Serves 8
Oven temperature 400°F, 200°C

PASTRY

1 cup/125 g flour

½ teaspoon baking powder

⅓ cup/90 g butter or shortening, cut into pieces

1½ tablespoons superfine sugar

1 egg yolk

½-1 tablespoon water

SPICY PUMPKIN FILLING

8 oz/250 g canned pumpkin

2 eggs, lightly beaten

½ cup/125 g dairy sour cream

½ cup/125 mL whipping cream

¼ cup/90 g light molasses or dark corn syrup

½ teaspoon ground nutmeg

½ teaspoon pumpkin pie spice

½ teaspoon ground cinnamon

1 To make pastry, sift flour and baking powder together into a bowl. Cut in butter or shortening until mixture resembles coarse bread crumbs, then stir in sugar. Make a well in the center of the flour mixture and mix in egg yolk and enough water to form a firm dough. Turn dough onto a lightly floured surface and knead lightly until smooth. Wrap pastry in plastic wrap and refrigerate for 30 minutes.

2 To make filling, place pumpkin, eggs, sour cream, cream, molasses or corn syrup, nutmeg, pie spice and cinnamon in a mixing bowl and beat until smooth and well combined.

3 Roll out pastry and line a greased 9 in/23 cm fluted tart pan with removable base. Spoon filling into pastry shell. Bake for 20 minutes then reduce oven temperature to 325°F/160°C and bake for 25-30 minutes longer or until filling is set and pastry golden. Stand in pan for 5 minutes before removing. Serve hot, warm or cold with whipped cream, if desired.

1 To make filling, place apricots, sugar, nutmeg and cinnamon in a bowl and mix to combine.

2 Spoon filling into a greased 6-cup/1.5 liter casserole. Roll out pastry to 1/8 in/3 mm thick. Mark center of pastry and cut four 4 in/10 cm slits, crossing at the center. Place pastry over filling and trim edges 1/4 in/5 mm wider than rim of casserole. Fold back flaps of pastry from center of pie. Make a large scalloped edge by placing your thumb against the inside pastry edge and molding the pastry around it with fingers of other hand.

3 Bake pie for 20-30 minutes or until pastry is golden and cooked through.

APRICOT COBBLER

Serves 6
Oven temperature 400°F, 200°C

1/2 quantity Shortbread Pastry (see page 160)

APRICOT FILLING
3 x 14 oz/440 g cans apricot halves, drained and sliced

1/4 cup/45 g packed brown sugar

1/2 teaspoon ground nutmeg

1/2 teaspoon ground cinnamon

PEAR AND FIG TART

Serves 8
Oven temperature 425°F, 220°C

HAZELNUT PASTRY
2 cups/250 g flour, sifted

1/3 cup/45 g finely chopped hazelnuts (filberts)

1 teaspoon pumpkin pie spice

3/4 cup/1 1/2 sticks/185 g butter or shortening, chilled and cut into small cubes

1 egg yolk, lightly beaten with a few drops of vanilla

4-5 tablespoons water, chilled

PEAR AND FIG FILLING
4 pears, peeled, cored and quartered

1/3 cup/90 g butter

4 oz/125 g dried figs, chopped

1/2 cup/90 g packed brown sugar

1/2 cup/125 mL honey or light molasses

1/2 cup/125 mL water

1/2 teaspoon vanilla

1/2 cup/60 g flour

1 egg, lightly beaten

1 To make pastry, place flour, hazelnuts (filberts) and pie spice in a bowl and cut in butter or shortening until the mixture resembles fine bread crumbs. Mix in egg yolk mixture and enough water to form a soft dough. Turn dough onto a lightly floured surface and knead lightly until smooth. Wrap dough in plastic wrap and refrigerate for 30 minutes.

2 Roll out pastry on a lightly floured surface and line a 1 3/4 in/4.5 cm deep, lightly greased 9 in/23 cm fluted tart with removable base. Refrigerate for 15 minutes. Line pastry shell with parchment paper, fill with uncooked rice and bake for 10 minutes, then remove rice and paper and cook for 10 minutes longer.

3 To make filling, cut each pear quarter into four slices. Melt 3 tablespoons/45 g of the butter in a skillet, add pears and cook for 4-5 minutes. Remove pears from pan and arrange in pastry shell. Sprinkle figs over pears.

4 Place sugar, honey or molasses, water, vanilla and remaining butter in a saucepan and cook over a medium heat, stirring, until sugar dissolves. Bring to the boil and simmer for 2 minutes.

5 Remove pan from heat and set aside to cool for 15 minutes, then beat in flour and egg. Pour over pears and figs and bake at 350°F/180°C for 50-55 minutes or until filling is firm. Serve warm.

MUSHROOM AND CHICKEN POT PIE

Serves 8
Oven temperature 400°F, 200°C

2 tablespoons/30 g butter

1 lb/500 g boneless skinned chicken breast halves

1 egg, lightly beaten

SOUR CREAM PASTRY
2¼ cups/280 g flour, sifted

½ cup/1 stick/125 g butter or shortening, chilled

¾ cup/185 g dairy sour cream

MUSHROOM SAUCE
¼ cup/½ stick/60 g butter

8 oz/250 g button mushrooms, sliced

¼ cup/30 g flour

1¼ cups/315 mL chicken stock

2 tablespoons finely chopped fresh parsley

⅓ cup/90 mL light cream (half-and-half)

2 tablespoons white wine

freshly ground black pepper

1   To make pastry, place flour into a large bowl. Cut in butter until mixture resembles coarse bread crumbs. Stir in sour cream and mix to form a soft dough. Turn dough onto a lightly floured surface and knead briefly. Wrap pastry in plastic wrap and refrigerate for 30 minutes.

2   Melt butter in a skillet, add chicken and cook for 4-5 minutes each side. Remove chicken from pan. Set aside to cool, then cut into cubes.

3   To make sauce, melt butter in a large saucepan, add mushrooms and cook over a medium heat, stirring, for 4-5 minutes or until soft. Remove mushrooms from pan using a slotted spoon and drain on paper towels.

4   Add flour to pan and cook, stirring, for 1 minute. Remove pan from heat and gradually blend in stock. Cook over a medium heat, stirring constantly, until mixture boils and thickens. Stir in parsley, cream, wine and mushrooms. Season to taste with black pepper. Set aside to cool.

5   Roll out two-thirds of pastry, and line the bottom and sides of a 2 in/5 cm deep, greased 8 in/20 cm quiche dish or casserole.

6   Fill pastry shell with alternate layers of chicken and sauce. Roll out remaining pastry to fit top of pie. Brush edges of pastry with water, cover filling with pastry top. Trim edges, then make slits in top of pie to allow steam to escape. Brush top with egg and bake for 25-35 minutes or until golden.

Mushroom and Chicken Pot Pie, Pear and Fig Tart (page 161)

NUT MILLEFEUILLES

Serves 6
Oven temperature 400°F, 200°C

1 sheet prerolled frozen puff pastry, thawed

confectioners' sugar

COCONUT FILLING
2 egg yolks

2 tablespoons superfine sugar

4 teaspoons cornstarch

¹/₂ teaspoon vanilla

¹/₂ cup/125 mL whipping cream

¹/₂ cup/125 mL coconut milk

¹/₃ cup/30 g grated dry coconut

NUT FILLING
¹/₃ cup/45 g finely chopped unsalted macadamia or brazil nuts

2 tablespoons dairy sour cream

2 tablespoons packed brown sugar

2 teaspoons dark rum

1 Roll out pastry to a 10 in/25 cm square and cut out nine rounds using a 3 in/7.5 cm cutter. Place on greased baking sheets and bake for 10 minutes or until puffed and golden brown. Cool on a wire rack.

2 To make Coconut Filling, place egg yolks, sugar, cornstarch and vanilla in a bowl and beat to combine. Place cream and coconut milk in a saucepan and bring just to the boil. Remove pan from heat and gradually whisk cream mixture into egg mixture. Return mixture to pan and cook over a low heat, stirring constantly, until mixture thickens and coats the back of a wooden spoon. Stir in coconut. Cover surface of custard with plastic wrap and set aside to cool.

3 To make Nut Filling, place nuts, sour cream, sugar and rum in a bowl and mix until well combined. Set aside.

4 To assemble millefeuilles, carefully split each pastry round into two layers. Spread one round with Coconut Filling, top with another pastry round, then spread with Nut Filling and finish with a final layer of pastry. Repeat with remaining pastry layers and fillings. To serve, dust with confectioners' sugar.

Cook's tip: If unsalted macadamia nuts are unavailable you can use salted macadamia nuts that have been rinsed under cold running water then dried in the oven for 10 minutes at 300°F/150°C. Take care not to toast the nuts when drying.

CHERRY AND APPLE TART

1 To make filling, melt butter in a skillet, add apples and cook for 3-4 minutes. Remove pan from heat and set aside to cool.

2 Arrange apples and cherries over bottom of pastry shell. Sprinkle with cinnamon. Place eggs, cream, sugar, flour and vanilla in a bowl and beat until smooth. Pour egg mixture over fruit. Bake tart for 30-35 minutes or until filling is set. Serve warm.

Serves 8
Oven temperature 375°F, 190°C

1 x 9 in/23 cm Sweet Pastry Shell (see page 169)
CHERRY FILLING
2 tablespoons/30 g butter
2 apples, cored, peeled and sliced
14 oz/440 g pitted tart red cherries, well drained
1 teaspoon ground cinnamon
2 eggs, lightly beaten
1/2 cup/125 mL whipping cream
1/3 cup/60 g packed brown sugar
4 teaspoons flour
1 teaspoon vanilla

CORNISH PASTIES

1 To make pastry, place butter and lard in a bowl and mix well to combine. Cover and refrigerate until firm. Place flour in a large bowl. Chop butter mixture into small pieces and cut into flour until mixture resembles coarse bread crumbs. Mix in enough water to form a soft dough. Turn dough onto a lightly floured surface and knead briefly. Wrap pastry in plastic wrap and refrigerate for 30 minutes.

2 To make filling, place beef, onion, potato, turnip, parsley, Worcestershire sauce and black pepper to taste in a bowl and mix well to combine.

3 Roll out pastry on a lightly floured surface and using an upturned saucer as a guide cut out six 6 in/15 cm rounds. Divide filling between pastry rounds. Brush edges with water and fold the pastry rounds in half and upwards to enclose filling, making edges meet at the top.

4 Press edges together to seal, then flute between finger and thumb. Place pasties on a greased baking sheet, brush with egg and bake for 15 minutes. Reduce oven temperature to 325°F/160°C and bake for 20 minutes or until golden. Serve hot, warm or cold.

Makes 6
Oven temperature 425°F, 220°C

PASTRY
1/4 cup/1/2 stick/60 g butter, softened
1/4 cup/60 g lard, softened
2 cups/250 g flour, sifted
1/3 cup/90 mL cold water
1 egg, lightly beaten
BEEF AND VEGETABLE FILLING
8 oz/250 g lean ground beef
1 small onion, grated
1 potato, shredded
1/2 small turnip, shredded
2 tablespoons finely chopped fresh parsley
1 tablespoon Worcestershire sauce
freshly ground black pepper

OLD ENGLISH PORK PIE

Serves 8
Oven temperature 500°F, 250°C

PASTRY
3 cups/375 g flour, sifted

1 teaspoon salt

$^1/_2$ cup/125 g lard or shortening

1 cup/250 mL water

1 egg yolk, lightly beaten with 1 tablespoon water

FILLING
3 lb/1.5 kg lean boneless pork, cut into $^1/_4$ in/5 mm cubes

$^1/_2$ teaspoon ground sage

freshly ground black pepper

2 cups/500 mL canned chicken or beef consommé

1 To make pastry, place flour and salt in a bowl and make a well in the center. Place lard or shortening and water in a saucepan and cook over a medium heat, stirring, until lard melts and mixture boils. Pour boiling liquid into flour and mix to form a firm dough. Knead pastry lightly until smooth. Cover and set aside to stand for 10 minutes.

2 Lightly knead two-thirds of pastry until pliable. Roll out to line bottom and sides of a 3 in/7.5 cm deep, greased 8 in/20 cm springform pan and bake for 15 minutes. Remove from oven. Set aside to cool.

3 To make filling, place pork, sage and black pepper to taste in a bowl and mix to combine. Pack pork mixture into pastry shell. Brush edges with a little of the egg yolk mixture.

4 Knead remaining pastry, then roll out to a circle large enough to cover pie. Place pastry over filling, trim pastry and press top to pastry shell. Cut a 1 in/2.5 cm circle from center of pastry. Brush pastry with remaining egg yolk mixture and bake for 30 minutes. Reduce oven temperature to 325°F/160°C and bake for 1$^1/_2$ hours. Remove any juices that appear in the hole during cooking. Cool pie in pan for 2 hours. Place chicken consommé in a saucepan and heat until melted. Cool slightly, then gradually pour into pie through hole in the top. Cool. Refrigerate pie overnight before cutting into wedges to serve.

*From left: Cornish Pasties (page 165),
Potato, Egg and Leek Pies,
Old English Pork Pie*

POTATO, EGG AND LEEK PIES

1 To make filling, melt butter in a skillet, add leeks and cook over a low heat, stirring, for 3-4 minutes or until soft. Stir in garlic and curry powder and cook, stirring, for 1 minute. Remove pan from heat. Set aside.

2 Chop potatoes. Add to leek mixture. Add chopped eggs, asparagus, parsley, sour cream, cheese and egg yolks and black pepper to taste. Mix to combine. Set aside to cool.

3 Line bottom and sides of eight greased metal individual pie dishes or muffin cups using two-thirds of the pastry. Cut remaining pastry to fit top of pies. Spoon filling into pie dishes and brush pastry edges with egg and top with pie lids. Press edges together to seal. Make a slit on the top of each pie using a sharp knife. Brush tops of pies with egg and bake for 15 minutes or until golden brown.

Makes 8 individual pies
Oven temperature 425°F, 220°C

3 sheets prerolled frozen puff pastry, thawed

1 egg, lightly beaten

POTATO AND LEEK FILLING

2 tablespoons/30 g butter

4 leeks, sliced

2 cloves garlic, crushed

2 teaspoons curry powder

6 potatoes, cooked until tender

4 eggs, hard-cooked and chopped

22 oz/700 g canned asparagus cuts, drained

3 tablespoons chopped fresh parsley

²/₃ cup/170 g dairy sour cream

1 cup/125 g shredded cheese

2 egg yolks, lightly beaten

freshly ground black pepper

1 egg, lightly beaten

caraway seeds

CARAMEL APPLE PIE

Serves 8
Oven temperature 400°F, 200°C

1 x 9 in/23 cm Sweet Pastry Shell (see page 169)

CARAMEL APPLE FILLING

1¼ cups/220 g packed brown sugar

¼ cup/60 mL water

1 cup/250 mL sweetened condensed milk

1 cup/250 mL whipping cream

4 egg yolks, beaten

4 tart green apples, cored, peeled and cut into thin slices

3 tablespoons/45 g butter

1   To make filling, place 1 cup/170 g of the brown sugar and water in a saucepan and mix to combine. Bring to simmering over a low heat, without stirring. Continue simmering, without stirring, for 7 minutes or until mixture thickens and is toffee-like. Remove pan from heat and set aside to cool for 10 minutes.

2   Whisk condensed milk and cream into toffee mixture. Then whisk in egg yolks. Spoon mixture into pastry shell and bake at 350°F/180°C for 10 minutes, remove pie from oven and set aside to cool to room temperature.

3   Place apple slices in a, lightly greased 8 in/20 cm round cake pan, sprinkle with remaining brown sugar and dot with butter. Bake at 350°F/180°C for 15 minutes or until apples are tender. Remove apples from oven and set aside to cool. Arrange apples on top of pie and decorate with whipped cream, if desired.

PEAR AND CREAM TART

Serves 8
Oven temperature 400°F, 200°C

PASTRY

2 cups/250 g flour

pinch salt

½ cup/1 stick/125 g unsalted (sweet) butter, chilled, cut into cubes

1 egg yolk

¼ cup/60 g superfine sugar

iced water

PEAR FILLING

5 firm pears, cored, peeled and halved

2 tablespoons lemon juice

⅓ cup/75 g superfine sugar

⅓ cup/90 mL whipping cream

⅛ teaspoon almond extract

1   To make pastry, place flour, salt, butter, egg yolk and sugar in a food processor or blender and process until mixture resembles coarse bread crumbs. With machine running, slowly add iced water until mixture forms a firm dough. Turn dough onto a lightly floured surface and knead briefly. Wrap pastry in plastic wrap and refrigerate for 30 minutes.

2   Roll out pastry to fit a lightly greased 12 in/30 cm fluted tart pan with removable base. Line pastry shell with parchment paper, fill with uncooked rice and place in freezer for 20 minutes. Bake for 10 minutes, then remove rice and paper and bake for 10 minutes longer.

3   For filling, brush pears with lemon juice, arrange cut side down in pastry shell and sprinkle with sugar. Bake for 20 minutes or until pears begin to soften.

4   Place cream and almond extract in a small bowl and mix to combine. Pour cream mixture over pears and bake for 15 minutes. Allow tart to stand for 5 minutes before removing from pan and serving.

Cook's tip: The amount of cream you use will depend on the depth of your tart pan. There will be pear juices after the initial cooking and the cream mingles with juices.

1   Place flour and sugar in a bowl and mix to combine. Using two knives or a pastry blender, cut in butter until mixture resembles fine bread crumbs. Stir in iced water a little at a time until a firm dough forms. Turn dough onto a lightly floured surface and knead briefly. Wrap pastry in plastic wrap and refrigerate for 30 minutes.

2   Roll out pastry to fit a lightly greased 9 in/23 cm fluted tart pan with removable base. Line pastry shell with parchment paper, fill with uncooked rice and bake for 10 minutes. Remove rice and paper and bake for 5 minutes longer or until pastry is golden. Use pastry shell as desired.

SWEET PASTRY SHELL

2¹/₂ cups/315 g flour

1 tablespoon superfine sugar

³/₄ cup/1¹/₂ sticks/185 g unsalted (sweet) butter, chilled, cut into small cubes

¹/₄-¹/₂ cup/60-125 mL iced water

1   To make filling, sprinkle gelatin over orange juice in a heatproof bowl set over a saucepan of simmering water and heat, stirring constantly, for 3-4 minutes or until gelatin dissolves. Remove bowl from heat and set aside to cool.

2   Place custard and cream in a bowl and mix to combine. Stir cooled gelatin mixture and liqueur into custard mixture. Pour into pastry shell and refrigerate for 30 minutes or until set.

3   Arrange kiwifruit, raspberries, peach and passion fruit attractively on custard and brush with warm jam. Set aside for 30 minutes or until glaze is set.

GLAZED FRUIT TART

Serves 8

1 x 9 in/23 cm Sweet Pastry Shell (see above)

FRUIT AND CUSTARD FILLING
2 teaspoons unflavored gelatin

¹/₄ cup/60 mL orange juice

1¹/₂ cups/375 mL prepared custard

¹/₂ cup/125 mL whipping cream

2 tablespoons orange-flavored liqueur

2 kiwifruit

8 oz/250 g raspberries

1 large peach, pitted, peeled and thinly sliced

1 passion fruit

¹/₄ cup/75 g apricot jam, warmed

THE CAKE STAND

The cake stand at a street market or fund raiser, with its wonderful array of goodies, is always popular and profitable. The cakes, cookies and bars in this chapter have been especially chosen because of their suitability for such events.

Honey Malt Bars (172), Hazelnut Fingers (page 173),
Orange Shortbread (page 176), Sesame Fruit Fingers (page 172),
Almond Cookies (page 173), Chocolate Chip Cookies (page 176)

Honey Malt Bars

Makes 20 bars
Oven temperature 350°F, 180°C

2 cups/250 g self-rising flour, sifted

1 cup/90 g rolled oats

1 cup/90 g grated dry coconut

8 oz/250 g malted wheat flake cereal, crushed

1 cup/170 g packed brown sugar

1 cup/2 sticks/250 g butter, melted

$^{1}/_{3}$ cup/125 g honey

MOCHA GLAZE

1 cup/155 g confectioners' sugar

2 teaspoons cocoa powder

2 teaspoons instant coffee powder

1 tablespoon/15 g butter, softened

1-2 tablespoons hot water

1 Place flour, rolled oats, coconut, wheat cereal and sugar in a large bowl and mix well to combine. Combine butter and honey and stir into dry ingredients.

2 Press mixture into a shallow, greased and lined 7 x 11 in/ 18 x 28 cm cake pan and bake for 35-40 minutes or until golden brown. Cool in pan.

3 To make glaze, sift confectioners' sugar, cocoa powder and instant coffee powder together into top of double boiler. Add butter, stir in water and mix to combine. Place over a saucepan of simmering water and heat, stirring constantly, to make glaze of an easy-to-spread consistency. Spread glaze over baked layer. Allow glaze to set and cut into bars.

Sesame Fruit Fingers

Makes 20
Oven temperature 350°F, 180°C

6 oz/185 g untoasted granola

$^{2}/_{3}$ cup/60 g grated dry coconut

$^{1}/_{2}$ cup/75 g wholewheat flour, sifted and grits removed

2 oz/60 g pine nuts (pignola)

$^{3}/_{4}$ cup/125 g golden seedless raisins

3 tablespoons sesame seeds

$^{1}/_{2}$ cup/90 g packed brown sugar

$^{1}/_{2}$ cup/1 stick/125 g butter, melted and cooled

2 tablespoons honey or light molasses

2 eggs, lightly beaten

1 Place granola, coconut, flour, pine nuts (pignola), raisins, sesame seeds and sugar in a bowl and mix to combine. Combine butter, honey or molasses and eggs and stir into dry ingredients.

2 Press mixture into a shallow, greased and lined 7 x 11 in/ 18 x 28 cm cake pan and bake for 20-25 minutes. Cool in pan and cut into fingers.

ALMOND COOKIES

1   Place butter and sugar in a bowl and beat until light and fluffy. Beat in almond extract and egg, then fold in flour, self-rising flour, coconut and cherries. Cover and refrigerate for 2 hours.

2   Roll heaped teaspoons of mixture into balls. Dip one half of each ball in chopped almonds and arrange almond side up on greased baking sheets, spacing balls well apart. Flatten each ball slightly and bake for 12-15 minutes or until golden. Remove from oven and transfer to wire racks to cool.

Makes 36
Oven temperature 350°F, 180°C

$^1/_2$ cup/1 stick/125 g butter

1 cup/220 g superfine sugar

$^1/_2$ teaspoon almond extract

1 egg

1 cup/125 g flour, sifted

1 cup/125 g self-rising flour, sifted

$^1/_2$ cup/45 g grated dry coconut

$^1/_2$ cup/90 g candied cherries, chopped

$^3/_4$ cup/125 g almonds, chopped

HAZELNUT FINGERS

1   Place egg whites in a bowl and beat until soft peaks form. Gradually add sugar, beating well until mixture is thick and glossy.

2   Fold hazelnuts (filberts), almond extract, cornstarch and flour into egg white mixture. Spoon mixture into a pastry bag fitted with a large plain tube. Pipe 2 in/5 cm lengths of mixture onto greased baking sheets and bake for 10 minutes. Remove from oven and transfer to wire racks to cool.

3   Dip cookie ends in melted chocolate and place on aluminum foil to set.

Makes 45
Oven temperature 350°F, 180°C

3 egg whites

$^3/_4$ cup/170 g superfine sugar

$2^1/_4$ cups/250 g ground hazelnuts (filberts)

$^1/_2$ teaspoon almond extract

$^1/_4$ cup/30 g cornstarch, sifted

$^1/_4$ cup/30 g flour, sifted

4 oz/125 g semi-sweet cooking chocolate, melted and cooled

QUICK MIX FRUIT CAKE

Makes an 8 in/20 cm ring cake
Oven temperature 325°F, 160°C

½ cup/1 stick/125 g butter, melted

1½ lb/750 g diced mixed dried and candied fruits and peels

½ cup/90 g packed brown sugar

2 tablespoons raspberry jam

2 eggs, lightly beaten

½ cup/125 mL sweet sherry

¾ cup/90 g flour, sifted

3 tablespoons self-rising flour, sifted

¾ cup/125 g blanched almonds

⅓ cup/60 g candied cherries, halved

1   Place butter, fruit, sugar, jam, eggs, sherry, flour and self-rising flour in a bowl and mix to combine.

2   Spoon batter into a 3 in/7.5 cm deep greased straight-sided 8 in/20 cm tube cake pan. Arrange almonds and cherries decoratively on top of cake and bake for 1½ hours or until cooked when tested with a skewer. Stand in pan for 15 minutes before turning onto a wire rack to cool.

Cook's tip: Recipe can be baked in a greased and floured 6-cup ring mold, a 9 in/23 cm square cake pan or a 3 in/7.5 cm deep, 8 in/20 cm springform pan, if desired.

Below: Quick Mix Fruit Cake, Zucchini and Walnut Loaf (page 177)
Right: Cocoa Mocha Cake (page 177)

CHOCOLATE CHIP COOKIES

Makes 36
Oven temperature 350°F, 180°C

¹/₂ cup/1 stick/125 g butter or shortening

¹/₂ cup/100 g superfine sugar

¹/₂ cup/90 g packed brown sugar

1 egg

³/₄ cup/90 g flour, sifted

²/₃ cup/60 g grated dry or flaked coconut

4 oz/125 g semi-sweet chocolate chips

4 oz/125 g semi-sweet cooking chocolate, melted and cooled

1   Place butter or shortening, superfine sugar and brown sugar in a bowl and beat until light and fluffy. Beat in egg, then fold in flour, coconut and chocolate chips.

2   Drop teaspoons of mixture onto greased baking sheets, allowing room for spreading and bake for 15 minutes. Remove from oven and transfer to wire racks to cool.

3   Place melted chocolate in a plastic bag, snip off corner and pipe three lines across top of each cookie.

ORANGE ENGLISH SHORTBREAD

Makes 20 squares
Oven temperature 350°F, 180°C

1 cup/2 sticks/250 g butter

¹/₂ cup/100 g superfine sugar

1 tablespoon orange juice

1 teaspoon finely grated orange rind

2 cups/250 g flour

¹/₂ cup/60 g cornstarch

extra superfine sugar

1   Place butter and superfine sugar in a bowl and beat until light and fluffy. Beat in orange juice and orange rind. Sift flour and cornstarch together and fold into butter mixture.

2   Press mixture into a greased and lined 8 in/20 cm square cake pan. Mark into squares and prick with a fork. Sprinkle with extra sugar and bake for 40-45 minutes or until just golden. Cool in pan, then cut into squares.

ZUCCHINI AND WALNUT LOAF

1   Place butter or shortening, sugar and honey or molasses in a bowl and beat until light and fluffy. Beat in pie spice and eggs, then stir in zucchini and walnuts.

2   Sift wholewheat flour, baking powder, soda and self-raising flour together. Return grits to bowl. Fold flour mixture and buttermilk or soured milk, alternately, into zucchini mixture.

3   Spoon batter into a greased and floured 4¹/₂ x 8¹/₂ in/11 x 21 cm loaf pan and bake for 40-45 minutes or until cooked when tested with a skewer. Stand in pan for 5 minutes before turning onto a wire rack to cool.

Cook's tip: To make soured milk, stir 2 teaspoons cider vinegar into ¹/₂ cup milk and let stand until curdled, about 10 minutes.

Makes a 4¹/₂ x 8¹/₂ in/11 x 21 cm loaf
Oven temperature 350°F, 180°C

¹/₂ **cup/1 stick/125 g butter or shortening**

¹/₄ **cup/45 g packed brown sugar**

¹/₄ **cup/90 g honey or light molasses**

1 teaspoon pumpkin pie spice

2 eggs

3 zucchini, shredded

³/₄ **cup/75 g walnuts, chopped**

1¹/₂ **cups/230 g wholewheat flour**

¹/₂ **teaspoon baking powder**

¹/₂ **teaspoon baking soda**

¹/₂ **cup/60 g self-rising flour**

¹/₂ **cup/125 mL buttermilk or soured milk**

COCOA MOCHA CAKE

1   Place cocoa powder and boiling water in a bowl and mix to combine. Set aside to cool completely.

2   Place butter or shortening, sugar and jam in a bowl and beat until light and fluffy. Beat in eggs, one at a time, adding a little flour with each egg. Fold cocoa mixture and remaining flour, alternately, into butter mixture.

3   Pour batter into two greased and floured 8 in/20 cm round layer pans and bake for 35 minutes or until cooked when tested with a skewer. Stand in pans for 5 minutes before turning onto wire racks to cool.

4   To make frosting, place butter in a bowl and beat until light and fluffy. Add confectioners' sugar a little at a time, beating well after each addition. Place cocoa powder and instant coffee powder in a bowl and mix in milk to make a smooth paste. Whisk cocoa mixture into butter mixture.

5   Spread one layer of cake with some frosting. Top with second layer and spread top and sides of cake with remaining frosting. Decorate with candied cherries and silver dragees.

Makes two 8 in/20 cm round layers
Oven temperature 350°F, 180°C

³/₄ **cup/75 g cocoa powder**

1¹/₂ **cups/375 mL boiling water**

³/₄ **cup/1¹/₂ sticks/185 g butter or shortening**

1³/₄ **cups/390 g superfine sugar**

2 tablespoons raspberry jam

3 eggs

2¹/₃ **cups/300 g self-rising flour**

CHOCOLATE MOCHA FROSTING
¹/₂ **cup/1 stick/125 g butter**

2 cups/315 g confectioners' sugar

2 tablespoons cocoa powder, sifted

2 teaspoons instant coffee powder

2 tablespoons milk

DECORATION
candied cherries

silver dragees

FESTIVE ALMOND CAKE

Makes two 4$\frac{1}{2}$ x 8$\frac{1}{2}$ in/11 x 21 cm cakes
Oven temperature 300°F, 150°C

$\frac{3}{4}$ **cup/155 g candied apricots, halved**

$\frac{3}{4}$ **cup/155 g red candied cherries**

$\frac{3}{4}$ **cup/155 g green candied cherries**

$\frac{1}{2}$ **cup/90 g seeded raisins**

4 oz/125 g brazil nuts

$\frac{1}{2}$ **cup/100 g oz pitted prunes**

1$\frac{1}{4}$ cups/125 g pecans or walnuts

$\frac{3}{4}$ **cup/100 g ground almonds**

$\frac{1}{2}$ **teaspoon baking powder**

3 eggs

2 tablespoons honey

2 teaspoons vanilla

1   Place apricots, red cherries, green cherries, raisins, brazil nuts, prunes, pecans or walnuts, almonds and baking powder in a bowl and mix to combine.

2   Place eggs in a bowl and beat until thick and creamy. Beat in honey and vanilla, then pour egg mixture into fruit mixture and mix to combine.

3   Divide mixture between two greased and lined 4$\frac{1}{2}$ x 8$\frac{1}{2}$ in/11 x 21 cm loaf pans, pressing down firmly, and bake for 1$\frac{1}{2}$ hours. Allow cakes to cool in pans.

LAMINGTONS

1 Place butter or shortening, sugar and vanilla in a bowl and beat until light and fluffy. Beat in eggs one at a time, beating well after each addition.

2 Sift flour, self-rising flour and baking powder together. Fold flour mixture and milk, alternately, into butter mixture. Pour batter into a greased and floured 10½ x 12¾ in/26 x 32 cm jelly roll pan and bake for 30-35 minutes or until sponge springs back when touched with fingertips. Stand in pan for 5 minutes before turning onto a wire rack to cool.

3 To make glaze, sift confectioners' sugar and cocoa powder together into a large bowl and mix in sufficient water to make a glaze of a smooth coating consistency.

4 Cut cake into twelve squares. Dip each piece of cake in chocolate glaze to completely coat, then roll in coconut and place on parchment paper to set.

Cook's tip: To make coating the cake easier, place coconut and glaze in two shallow dishes or cake pans. Use tongs or two forks to dip the cake in the glaze, then place on a wire rack set over a sheet of paper and allow to drain for 2-3 minutes before rolling in the coconut.

Makes 12
Oven temperature 350°F, 180°C

¹/₂ cup/1 stick/125 g butter or shortening

³/₄ cup/170 g superfine sugar

1 teaspoon vanilla

2 eggs

1 cup/125 g flour

1 cup/125 g self-rising flour

1 teaspoon baking powder

¹/₂ cup/125 mL milk

CHOCOLATE GLAZE
3 cups/470 g confectioners' sugar

4 tablespoons cocoa powder

6-8 tablespoons boiling water

grated dry or sweetened flaked coconut

Left: Festive Almond Cake
Above: Lamingtons

WALNUT CRUNCHIES

Makes 18
Oven temperature 300°F, 150°C

¹/₂ cup/1 stick/125 g butter or shortening

²/₃ cup/170 g granulated brown (raw or demerara) sugar

2 tablespoons light molasses or honey

1 egg, lightly beaten

1 cup/90 g grated dry coconut

1¹/₂ cups/230 g wholewheat flour

¹/₂ teaspoon baking soda

18 walnut halves

1   Place butter or shortening in a saucepan and melt over a medium heat. Remove pan from heat. Stir in sugar, molasses or honey and egg. Add coconut, flour and baking soda and mix well to combine.

2   Take teaspoons of mixture and roll into balls. Place balls 1¹/₄ in/3 cm apart on greased baking sheets. Press a walnut half into top of each ball and flatten slightly. Bake for 30 minutes or until golden. Stand on sheets for 3-5 minutes before transferring to wire racks to cool.

SESAME CARAMELS

Makes 60

1 cup/170 g packed brown sugar

¹/₃ cup/90 g butter

2 tablespoons honey

¹/₃ cup/125 g corn syrup (light or dark)

¹/₂ cup/125 mL sweetened condensed milk

3 tablespoons sunflower seeds, chopped

5 oz/155 g sesame seeds, toasted

1   Place sugar, butter, honey, corn syrup and condensed milk in a saucepan and cook over a low heat, stirring, until sugar is dissolved. Slowly bring to the boil and cook, stirring constantly, for 7 minutes.

2   Stir in sunflower seeds and 3 tablespoons sesame seeds. Pour mixture into a shallow, aluminum foil-lined 7 x 11 in/ 18 x 28 cm cake pan. Set aside to cool to room temperature.

3   Cut caramel into four strips lengthwise, then fold each strip in half and roll into a ³/₄ in/2 cm diameter log. Roll each log in remaining sesame seeds and refrigerate for 1 hour. Cut into slices.

WHOLEWHEAT SCOTTISH SHORTBREAD

1   Place butter and sugar in a bowl and beat until light and fluffy. Sift wholewheat flour, flour, ground rice (rice flour) and wheat germ together, return grits to bowl. Stir flour mixture into butter mixture and mix to form a firm dough.

2   Turn dough onto a lightly floured surface and knead for 2 minutes or until smooth.

3   Roll dough out to 8 in/20 cm round. Place round on a lightly greased and floured baking sheet and using thumb and forefinger of one hand and forefinger of the other, pinch around edge, to give shortbread a decorative finish. Bake for 30-40 minutes or until lightly browned. Cool on sheet.

Makes 8 pieces
Oven temperature 325°F, 160°C

1 cup/2 sticks/250 g butter

¹/₂ cup/90 g packed brown sugar

1 cup/155 g wholewheat flour, sifted

1 cup/125 g flour, sifted

¹/₄ cup/45 g ground rice (rice flour)

3 tablespoons wheat germ

APRICOT FRUIT RING CAKE

1   Place butter or shortening and sugar in a bowl and beat until light and fluffy. Add eggs one at a time, beating well after each addition. Sift flour and pie spice together and mix into butter mixture. Add dried apricots, candied apricots, currants and pecans and mix well to combine.

2   Spoon batter into a greased 3 in/7.5 cm deep, straight-sided 8 in/20 cm tube pan and bake for 1¹/₂ hours or until cake is cooked when tested with a skewer. Cool in pan before turning out.

3   To make topping, place apricots in a bowl and pour over enough boiling water to cover then set aside to stand for 15 minutes. Drain and pat dry with paper towels. Place jam and brandy in a small saucepan and heat over a medium heat until almost boiling. Remove pan from heat and brush top of cake with half the jam mixture. Arrange apricots and pecans decoratively on top of cake, then brush with remaining jam mixture.

Cook's tip: Recipe can be baked in a 6-cup ring mold, an 8 in/20 cm springform pan or 2 in/5 cm deep, 9 in/23 cm square cake pan, if desired.

Makes an 8 in/20 cm ring cake
Oven temperature 300°F, 150°C

³/₄ cup/1¹/₂ sticks/185 g butter or shortening

¹/₂ cup/100 g superfine sugar

3 eggs

³/₄ cup/90 g flour

2 teaspoons pumpkin pie spice

1 lb/500 g dried apricots, chopped

²/₃ cup/125 g candied apricots, chopped

1²/₃ cup/250 g currants

2¹/₂ cups/250 g pecans, chopped

APRICOT TOPPING
15-20 dried apricots

3 tablespoons apricot jam

2 tablespoons brandy

20 pecan halves

GINGERBREAD FAMILY

Makes a family of four plus a cat and a dog
Oven temperature 350°F, 180°C

½ cup/1 stick/125 g butter or shortening

½ cup/90 g packed brown sugar

1 egg

1 cup/125 g flour

1½ cups/185 g self-rising flour

1 teaspoon baking soda

1 tablespoon ground ginger

2 tablespoons honey

DECORATOR ICING
1 egg white

1½ cups/250 g confectioners' sugar, sifted

a little lemon juice

food coloring

1   Place butter or shortening and sugar in a bowl and beat until light and fluffy. Beat in egg. Sift flour, self-rising flour, baking soda and ginger together and fold into butter mixture. Add honey and mix well to combine.

2   Turn dough onto a lightly floured surface and knead until soft, but not sticky. Wrap dough into plastic wrap and refrigerate for 30 minutes. Divide dough into four equal portions and roll out each portion to ⅛ in/3 mm thick.

3   Cut out shapes with gingerbread cookie cutters or make cardboard cutouts. Cut two large shapes (mother and father) and two small shapes (children). Using a spatula, carefully lift gingerbread figures onto a lightly greased baking sheet. Reroll remaining dough scraps and use to make a cat and a dog. Place cat and dog on baking sheet and bake for 10 minutes or until cooked. Cool on sheets.

4   To make icing, place egg white in a bowl and beat with a wooden spoon. Add confectioners' sugar a tablespoon at a time, beating well after each addition. When icing reaches piping consistency, stir in a few drops of lemon juice, then divide into small quantities and color as desired.

5   Spoon icing into small plastic bags and snip off one corner, then pipe facial features and clothes onto gingerbread shapes.

Right: Cashew Cookies (page 184),
Chocolate Almond Balls (page 185)
Far right: Gingerbread Family

ORANGE AND LIME YOGURT SYRUP CAKE

Makes an 8 in/20 cm ring cake
Oven temperature 350°F, 180°C

1/2 cup/1 stick/125 g butter or shortening

1 teaspoon finely grated lime rind

1 tablespoon finely grated orange rind

1 cup/220 g superfine sugar

3 eggs

1²/₃ cups/200 g self-rising flour, sifted

1/2 cup/125 g plain yogurt

LIME AND ORANGE SYRUP
2 tablespoons lime juice

3 tablespoons orange juice

3 tablespoons sugar

1   Place butter or shortening, lime rind and orange rind in a bowl and beat until light and creamy. Add sugar a little at a time and continue beating until light and fluffy.

2   Beat in eggs one a time, beating well after each addition. Fold flour and yogurt, alternately, into butter mixture. Spoon batter into a 3 in/7.5 cm deep, greased 8 in/20 cm fluted tube pan and bake for 30-35 minutes or until cooked when tested with a skewer. Stand in pan for 5 minutes before turning onto a wire rack placed on a tray.

3   To make syrup, place lime juice, orange juice and sugar in small saucepan and cook over a medium heat, stirring constantly, until sugar dissolves. Bring mixture to the boil, without stirring, and boil for 3 minutes. Remove pan from heat and pour hot syrup over hot cake. Set aside to cool.

CASHEW COOKIES

Makes 48
Oven temperature 350°F, 180°C

1/2 cup/1 stick/125 g butter or shortening

1/3 cup/75 g superfine sugar

1 teaspoon vanilla

1 egg yolk

1 cup/125 g flour, sifted

1/2 cup/60 g self-rising flour, sifted

2 tablespoons wheat germ

²/₃ cup/60 g unsalted cashews, toasted

1   Place butter or shortening and sugar in a bowl and beat until light and fluffy. Add vanilla and egg yolk and beat to combine.

2   Fold flour, self-rising flour and wheat germ into butter mixture. Turn dough onto a lightly floured surface and knead briefly. Shape into a log, wrap in plastic wrap and refrigerate for 30 minutes or until firm.

3   Slice dough into 1/4 in/5 mm slices and place on greased baking sheets. Press a cashew into the top of each cookie and bake for 10-12 minutes or until golden. Remove from oven and transfer to wire racks to cool.

SWEET POTATO QUICK BREAD

1   Place sweet potato and half the sugar in a skillet and cook over a medium heat, stirring frequently, for 4-5 minutes. Remove pan from heat and set aside.

2   Sift flour, cinnamon and nutmeg together into a bowl. Add remaining sugar and mix to combine. Make a well in the center of the dry ingredients and add vanilla, oil, egg yolks and baking soda mixture. Mix well to combine. Fold almonds, grated coconut and sweet potato (yam) mixture into batter.

3   Place egg whites in a bowl and beat until stiff peaks form. Fold egg white mixture into batter. Spoon batter into a greased and floured 4¹/₂ x 8¹/₂ in/11 x 21 cm loaf pan, sprinkle with shredded coconut and bake for 1¹/₄ hours or until cooked when tested with a skewer. Stand in pan for 5 minutes before turning onto a wire rack to cool.

Makes a 4¹/₂ x 8¹/₂ in/11 x 21 cm loaf
Oven temperature 350°F, 180°C

10 oz/315 g sweet potato (yam), shredded

1¹/₂ cups/250 g packed brown sugar

1¹/₂ cups/185 g flour, sifted

¹/₂ teaspoon ground cinnamon

1 teaspoon ground nutmeg

¹/₂ teaspoon vanilla

¹/₂ cup/125 mL vegetable oil

2 eggs, separated

1 teaspoon baking soda blended with 7 tablespoons water

³/₄ cup/125 g almonds, chopped

²/₃ cup/60 g grated dry coconut

²/₃ cup/30 g shredded dry coconut

CHOCOLATE ALMOND BALLS

1   Place cream and chocolate in a saucepan and cook over a low heat, stirring, until chocolate melts. Remove pan from heat and set aside to cool slightly. Stir in butter, cover and chill.

2   Using an electric mixer, beat chocolate mixture until soft peaks form. Return to the refrigerator and chill until firm.

3   Place almonds and rice cereal in a bowl and mix to combine. Shape teaspoons of chocolate mixture into balls and roll in almond mixture. Store in an airtight container in the refrigerator.

Makes 24

¹/₂ cup/125 mL whipping cream

4 oz/125 g semi-sweet cooking chocolate, chopped

1 tablespoon/15 g butter

¹/₃ cup/60 g almonds, finely chopped, toasted

1 cup/30 g crisp rice cereal, crushed

CHILDREN'S BIRTHDAY CAKES

*In a child's eyes, there is nothing to
beat the excitement of a birthday party, and
central to the party is the cake. In this chapter
you will find instructions for making
wonderfully imaginative birthday cakes.*

Circus Three (page 196)

LEO THE LION

1 Leo template (see page 228)

2 x 9 in/23 cm square cakes

1 quantity Butter Cream (see page 222)

food colorings; dark brown, caramel

1 oz/30 g Covering Fondant (see page 223) or purchased marzipan (almond paste)

2 dark brown candy-coated chocolates

1 large oval chocolate-coated candy

Enlarge template, using one of the techniques described on page 226. Cut out paper template and cut into two pieces – head and body. Using guide lines on template cut out waxed paper eyes.

CAKE CONSTRUCTION

1   Place one template on each cake. Using a sharp knife, cut around templates.

2   Place the cakes on a board and join pieces together using a little Butter Cream.

STEP-BY-STEP FROSTING

1   Color 4 oz/125 g Butter Cream dark brown. Divide remaining Butter Cream equally and color one portion caramel and the other portion a darker caramel.

2   Spread lighter caramel Butter Cream over top and sides of Leo.

3   Place templates over Butter Cream and using a skewer prick through template into Butter Cream to mark out facial features, arms and feet.

4   Spoon dark brown Butter Cream into a pastry bag fitted with a writing tube. Using holes as a guide, pipe in Leo's facial features, arms and feet. Using picture as a guide, pipe in dark brown outline.

5   Spoon one quarter of the darker caramel Butter Cream into a pastry bag fitted with a writing tube and pipe short lines all over Leo's body and head, excluding mane and end of tail. Using a skewer, fluff up the lines to give texture to Leo.

6   Spoon remaining darker caramel Butter Cream into a pastry bag fitted with a star tube and pipe Leo's mane and tail. To pipe mane and tail, start at the outside edge. Touch tube to cake and squeeze pastry bag firmly so that Butter Cream adheres to cake to leave a tapering strand. Continue piping strands until entire mane area is filled in. Using the same technique, fill in the end of Leo's tail.

FINISHING TOUCHES

1   Roll out Covering Fondant or marzipan on a surface lightly dusted with cornstarch and using paper eyes, cut out Leo's eyes. Using picture as a guide, position eyes.

2   Using pastry bag fitted with a writing tube, pipe dark brown outline around the eyes.

3   Position brown candy-coated chocolates on fondant.

4   Using picture as a guide, position oval chocolate nose.

TOBY THE TORTOISE

1 cake cooked in a 7 cup/1.75 liter pudding basin (see page 219)

4 cupcakes

1 lb/500 g Covering Fondant (see page 223)

food colorings; green, pink, caramel, black

apricot jam

1 egg white, beaten

1 round plain cookie

2 white flat round candies

2 in/5 cm piece licorice straw

No template is required to make Toby.

STEP-BY-STEP FROSTING

1 Color 12 oz/375 g of the fondant green, 2 oz/60 g pink, 2 oz/60 g beige (caramel) and remaining fondant black.

2 Roll out green fondant thinly on a surface lightly dusted with cornstarch. Using a 9 in/23 cm metal cake or tart pan as a guide, cut a circle. Reserve any leftover fondant. Brush pudding basin cake with melted apricot jam and place fondant over. Using the palms of the hands, smooth out fondant so that there are no air bubbles. Flute edges of Toby's shell using fingers dipped in cornstarch.

3 Roll out pink fondant thinly and using a ³/₄ in/2 cm round cutter, cut out spots. Brush each spot with egg white. Place spots decoratively on Toby's green shell.

4 Roll out beige fondant thinly. Cut beige fondant to fit over legs and head. Cut 3 of the cupcakes horizontally in half. Brush 4 of the halves and the remaining whole cupcake with melted jam. Place fondant over. Smooth to remove air bubbles.

5 Roll out a piece of green fondant thinly and cut a 6 in/15 cm circle. Brush cookie with melted jam and cover completely with green fondant circle. Smooth to remove air bubbles.

6 One of the remaining cupcake halves is the crown of Toby's hat (you can eat or discard the remaining half!). Roll out pink fondant to fit over cupcake. Brush cake with melted jam. Place fondant over. Smooth to remove air bubbles.

7 Roll out remaining green fondant and cut ¹/₂ in/1 cm circles to form spots on hat. Brush spots with beaten egg white and place around crown of hat.

CAKE CONSTRUCTION

1 Place main part of Toby on a board and using picture as a guide, position feet and head.

2 Brush bottom of fondant covered cookie with egg white and position on Toby's head to form brim of hat.

3 Brush bottom of crown with beaten egg white. Place on brim.

FINAL TOUCHES

1 Roll out black fondant thinly and cut two small circles. Brush with egg white and using picture as a guide, position white sweets.

2 Brush back of each white candy with beaten egg white and position as eyes on Toby's head. Position licorice as Toby's mouth.

Leo the Lion (page 188)

Toby the Tortoise (page 189)

Looney Tunes

Alphabet template (see page 232)
two 7 x 11 in/18 x 28 cm slab cakes
raspberry jam
1 quantity Butter Cream (see page 222)
food colorings; red, green, blue, yellow
red candy-coated chocolates
green candy-coated chocolates
Happy Birthday ribbon

Trace required letters for message and adjust size, (see page 226).

CAKE CONSTRUCTION
Sandwich cakes together using a little raspberry jam and place on a covered board.

STEP-BY-STEP FROSTING
1   Color 2 oz/60 g Butter Cream red, 2 oz/60 g green, 2 oz/60 g blue. Color remaining Butter Cream yellow.

2   Spread top and sides of cake with yellow Butter Cream. Place tracing of letters on cake surface and using a skewer, prick through to mark message on Butter Cream.

4   Spoon red, blue and green Butter Cream into separate pastry bags fitted with writing tubes and using holes and picture as guides, pipe in red, blue and green writing and music.

5   Spoon remaining yellow Butter Cream into a pastry bag fitted with a star tube and pipe a shell border around the top and bottom of cake.

FINISHING TOUCHES
1   Using picture as a guide, position candy-coated chocolates to form the notes of the music.

2   Position Happy Birthday ribbon around cake.

SOLDIER BOY

Enlarge template, using one of the techniques described on page 226. Cut out paper template, then cut template into three through dotted lines.

CAKE CONSTRUCTION

1 Place one template piece on each cake. Using a sharp knife, cut around templates. Place cakes on a board and join using a little Butter Cream.

2 Place template over cake and using a skewer, prick through template into cake to mark division between clothes.

STEP-BY-STEP FROSTING

1 Color 2 oz/60 g Butter Cream yellow, 2 oz/60 g light grey, 4 oz/125 g black, 4 oz/125 g dark grey and 4 oz/125 g red. Leaving remaining Butter Cream plain.

2 Spread red Butter Cream over sides and top of jacket area.

3 Spread dark grey Butter Cream over sides and top of pants area. Spread black Butter Cream over sides and top of boots and hat area. Spread light grey Butter Cream over sides and top of gun area.

4 Spread plain Butter Cream over sides and top of face and hands areas.

5 Spoon black Butter Cream into a pastry bag fitted with a large writing tube and pipe a small quantity into belt area. Spread frosting out to fill belt area.

6 Spoon remaining dark grey Butter Cream into a pastry bag fitted with a star tube and pipe in the hat. To pipe hat, start at the outside edge, touch the tube to the cake and squeeze pastry bag firmly so that the Butter Cream adheres to the cake, then pull away from cake to leave a tapering strand. Continue piping strands to fill hat area.

7 Spoon yellow Butter Cream into a pastry bag fitted with a writing tube and using picture as a guide, pipe in lapel on jacket and belt features.

8 Using picture as a guide, pipe black Butter Cream outline and features of soldier boy.

FINISHING TOUCHES

Position round red candy as nose and yellow boiled candies as buttons. Position moustache as shown in picture.

---

1 Soldier Boy template (see page 229)

three 7 x 11 in/18 x 28 cm slab cakes

1 quantity Butter Cream (see page 222)

food colorings; yellow, light grey, black, dark grey, red

1 candy-coated round red chocolate

4 yellow O-shaped boiled candies

1 false moustache

Looney Tunes (page 192)

Soldier Boy (page 193)

SCOOPS OF ICE CREAM

1 jelly roll

6 cupcakes, halved horizontally

1 quantity Fluffy Frosting (see page 222)

food colorings; yellow, blue, pink, caramel

crushed nuts

1 raspberry jube

No template is required to make this cake.

CAKE CONSTRUCTION

1   Lay jelly roll flat and mark the center at one end of the roll. Using a sharp knife, cut a line from each side to the center to form a cone shape.

2   Place cake on a covered board.

STEP-BY-STEP FROSTING

1   Divide frosting into five portions. Color one portion yellow, one bright blue, one dark pink and one caramel. Leave remaining portion white.

2   Spread caramel frosting over jelly roll and, using a ruler, mark crisscrossing diagonal lines to resemble a cone.

3   Spread three cupcake halves with blue frosting, three with yellow frosting, three with white frosting and three with pink frosting.

4   Using picture as a guide, position frosted cakes as scoops of ice cream above the cone.

FINISHING TOUCHES

Position raspberry jube on top of ice cream. Sprinkle top of ice cream with crushed nuts.

CIRCUS THREE

2 x 8³/₄ in/22 cm ring cakes

¹/₂ quantity Fluffy Frosting (see page 222)

¹/₂ quantity Butter Cream (see page 222)

food coloring, yellow

toy train, with provision for candles (available from novelty stores, supermarkets and cake decorator supply shops)

4 toy clowns

For cake construction see page 208.

STEP-BY-STEP FROSTING

1   Color 2 oz/60 g Butter Cream pale lemon and 2 oz /60 g dark yellow.

2   Spread top of cake with frosting and fluff up with a fork.

3   Spoon pale lemon Butter Cream into one side of a pastry bag fitted with a leaf tube. Spoon dark yellow Butter Cream into other side of pastry bag. Squeeze pastry bag onto a board until both colors flow through tube to give a two-toned effect.

4   Pipe wavy vertical lines on side of cake, starting from bottom and working up to top of cake. Holding tube to one side, squeeze wavy lines on top and bottom edges of cake.

FINISHING TOUCHES

Position train, candles and clowns on top of cake as shown in picture.

COLA BOTTLE

Enlarge template, using one of the techniques described on page 226. Cut out paper template.

CAKE CONSTRUCTION

1 Place jelly roll on template and using a sharp knife, cut to make shape of a cola bottle.

2 Position jam rollette for neck of bottle and using template as a guide, cut to shape.

3 Place cakes on a board and join together using a little Butter Cream.

4 Place template on cake and using a skewer, prick through template to mark in froth line.

STEP-BY-STEP FROSTING

1 Place 4 oz/125 g Butter Cream in a bowl and set aside. Color remaining Butter Cream brown using cocoa powder and brown food coloring until desired color is achieved.

2 Using picture and holes as a guide, spread brown Butter Cream over sides and top of bottle.

3 Place template over chocolate Butter Cream and using a skewer, prick through template and mark in bottle label.

4 Spread plain Butter Cream over froth area. Spoon remaining Butter Cream into a pastry bag fitted with a writing tube and pipe in bottle label.

FINISHING TOUCHES

Using picture as a guide, position straw in the top of cola bottle.

1 Cola Bottle template (see page 230)
1 jelly roll
1 jam rollette
1 quantity Butter Cream (see page 222)
cocoa powder
food coloring, brown
1 straw

Scoops of Ice Cream (page 196), Cola Bottle (page 197)

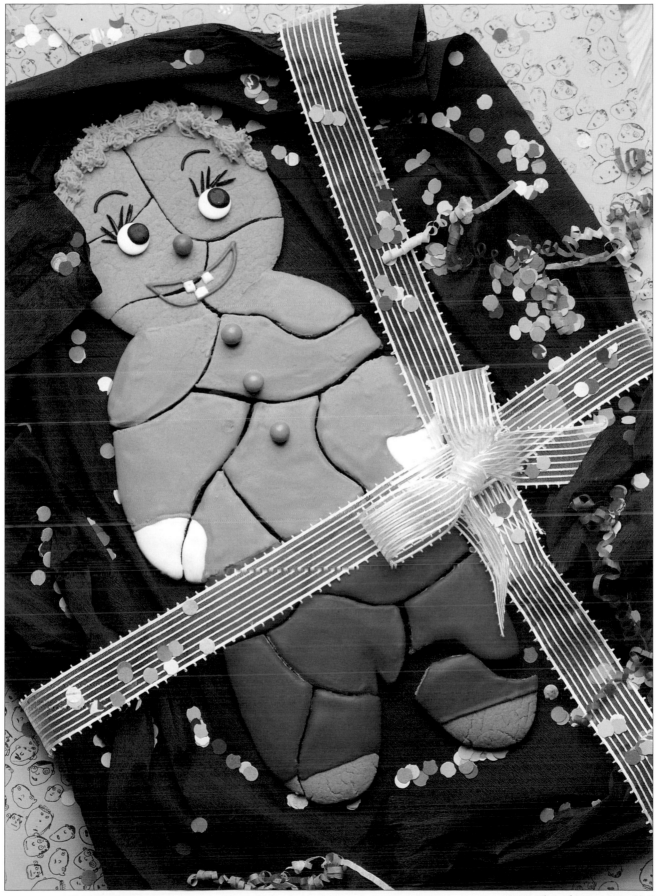

Gingerbread Man (page 204)

RED RIDING HOOD

1 cake cooked in a 7 cup/1.75 liter pudding basin

12 in/30 cm doll (available from toy shops)

8 oz/250 g Covering Fondant (see page 223)

1 quantity thick Royal Icing (see page 223)

food coloring, red

1 egg white, lightly beaten

small bunch fresh or dried flowers

No template is required to make Red Riding Hood.

CAKE CONSTRUCTION

1   Place cake upside down on a covered cake board. Cut center out of cake to fit doll.

2   Position doll in center of cake and pack around it with cut-out cake.

STEP-BY-STEP FROSTING

1   Color fondant red. Roll fondant out thinly to a 5$\frac{1}{2}$ x 13 in/14 x 33 cm rectangle. Measure in 4$\frac{1}{4}$ in/10.5 cm on each long edge, then 2 in/5 cm down short side.

2   Using a sharp knife and starting from long edge mark, cut away fondant down to mark on short side, curving as you cut to form front of cape.

3   Brush cake and back of doll with egg white. Place fondant over cake and back of doll, starting with tapered piece at neck edge, crimping in with fingertips to fit. Smooth remaining fondant over cake, leaving 6$\frac{1}{2}$ in/16 cm uncovered on front of doll.

4   Roll out fondant scraps and cut a piece of 3$\frac{1}{4}$ x 5$\frac{1}{2}$ in/8 x 14 cm for hood. Brush shorter side with egg white and position on back of neck, crimping with fingertips to fit. Bring wider part up over head, working with fingertips to form hood.

5   Color 2 oz/60 g Royal Icing red to match cape. Set aside. Spoon remaining Royal Icing into a pastry bag fitted with a leaf tube. Starting at the bottom front of cake, pipe wavy overlapping lines all over front of cake and up over waist, chest and top part of arms of doll.

FINISHING TOUCHES

1   Spoon red Royal Icing into a pastry bag fitted with a writing tube and pipe around the edge of Red Riding Hood's cape.

2   Using picture as a guide, position flowers in doll's hand.

PARCEL CAKE

No template is required for this cake.

CAKE CONSTRUCTION
Trim top of cake so that it is level. Turn upside down and place on a 9 in/23 cm square board.

STEP-BY-STEP FROSTING
1   Brush top and sides of cake with apricot jam.

2   Roll out Covering Fondant thinly to a 14 in/34 cm square. Place over cake and smooth out with palms of hands to remove air bubbles. Trim any excess fondant from around the base of the cake.

3   Cut rice paper to fit the top and sides of the cake. Using food coloring and picture as a guide, paint words and pattern onto rice paper.

4   Attach rice paper to cake using a little Royal Icing.

FINISHING TOUCHES
Tie a bow for the top of the parcel and position ribbon around the parcel and bow on top as shown in the picture.

1 x 9 in/23 cm square cake

1 lb/500 g Covering Fondant (see page 223)

1/2 quantity Royal Icing (see page 223)

food colorings; blue, purple

apricot jam, melted

6 sheets rice paper

2 1/2 yds/2 m blue ribbon

WONDERFUL ONE

two 3¼ x 10½ in/8 x 26 cm bar cakes

1 quantity Butter Cream (see page 222)

food coloring; purple, green

1 cup/90 g grated dry coconut

4 in/10 cm square piece gingham fabric

1 candle

3 small toy bears

For cake construction see page 208. Reserve cut-off cake.

STEP-BY-STEP FROSTING

1   Color 2 oz/60 g Butter Cream purple. Color remaining Butter Cream green.

2   Spread sides and top of cake with green Butter Cream.

3   Color coconut green. Sprinkle top and sides of cake with colored coconut.

FINISHING TOUCHES

1   Fray edges of gingham square and place as shown in picture.

2   Cut reserved cake to form a small round cake. Spread with purple Butter Cream, insert candle and position on tablecloth as shown in picture.

3   Using picture as a guide, position bears around small cake on tablecloth.

Red Riding Hood (page 200)

Parcel Cake (page 201), Hooray Hooray Cake (page 211), Happy Birthday Cake (page 210)

GINGERBREAD MAN

1 Gingerbread Man template (see page 231)

ingredients for gingerbread dough (see page 182)

1 quantity Royal Icing (see page 223)

food colorings; black, pink, blue, yellow

4 oz/125 g Covering Fondant (see page 223)

2 white flat round candies

1 licorice strap or whip

3 green round candy-coated chocolates

1 pink round candy

Enlarge template, using one of the techniques described on page 226. Cut out paper template.

CAKE CONSTRUCTION

1   Make up gingerbread dough according to recipe. Roll out thinly to ⅛ in/3 mm thickness. Place template over dough and using a sharp knife, cut around template. Place on a baking sheet and using picture and number of children you are going to have at the party as a guide, mark out jigsaw pieces. Cut right through each piece using a sharp knife, but do not separate.

2   Bake at 400°F/200°C for 15-20 minutes or until golden. Using a sharp knife, cut through pieces again and separate gently. Stand on sheet for 5 minutes before transferring to a wire rack to cool.

STEP-BY-STEP FROSTING

1   Color 1 tablespoon Royal Icing black. Leave 2 oz/ 60 g Royal Icing white, color half the remaining Icing pink and the other half blue.

2   Using picture as a guide, coat each piece of the shirt of the Gingerbread Man blue. Remember to leave hand areas uncoated. Then coat each piece of the pants pink. Remember to leave feet areas uncoated.

3   Using picture as a guide, coat hand areas white. Reassemble puzzle on a large covered board.

4   Color fondant yellow and press through a garlic press to make hair. Position hair on Gingerbread Man's head.

FINISHING TOUCHES

1   Spoon a little pink Royal Icing into a pastry bag fitted with a writing tube and pipe in mouth.

2   Position white candies as eyes, holding in place with a little Royal Icing. Spoon a little white Royal Icing into a pastry bag fitted with a writing tube and pipe in teeth.

3   Spoon black Royal Icing into a pastry bag fitted with a writing tube and pipe in eye features.

4   Cut licorice strap to make eyelashes and eyebrows and place as shown in picture. Position green candies as buttons on Gingerbread Man's shirt holding in place with a little Royal Icing. Position pink candy as Gingerbread Man's nose, holding in place with a little Royal Icing.

SWEET SEVEN

For cake construction see page 209.

STEP-BY-STEP FROSTING
1 Color Butter Cream blue.

2 Spread sides and top of cake with Butter Cream.

FINISHING TOUCHES
1 Mark diagonal lines 1 in/2.5 cm apart across the surface of the cake. Using picture as a guide, decorate cake with assorted candies.

2 Spoon remaining Butter Cream into a pastry bag fitted with a star tube and pipe a shell border around top outside edge of cake.

two $3^1/_4$ x $10^1/_2$ in/8 x 26 cm bar cakes
1 quantity Butter Cream (see page 222)
food coloring; blue
assorted candies for decoration

FENCING FOUR

For cake construction see page 208.

STEP-BY-STEP FROSTING
1 Color Butter Cream using cocoa and brown food coloring until desired color is achieved.

2 Spread Butter Cream over top and sides of cake. Using the edge of a ruler, mark in the fence markings.

FINISHING TOUCHES
Using picture as a guide, position brown candy-coated chocolates.

three $3^1/_4$ x $10^1/_2$ in/8 x 26 cm bar cakes
1 quantity Butter Cream (see page 222)
cocoa powder
food coloring, caramel
8 brown candy-coated chocolates

WHISTLING SIX

3¹/₄ x 10¹/₂ in/8 x 26 cm bar cake

8³/₄ in/22 cm ring cake

1 quantity Butter Cream (see page 222)

food colorings; blue, yellow, pink, orange, purple

blue candy sprinkles

yellow candy sprinkles

pink candy sprinkles

multi-colored candy sprinkles

multi-colored feathers

For cake construction see page 209.

STEP-BY-STEP FROSTING

1   Colour 3 oz/90 g Butter Cream bright blue, 3 oz/90 g bright yellow, 2 oz/60 g pink, 2 oz/60 g orange, 2 oz/60 g purple. Leave remaining Butter Cream plain.

2   Using picture as a guide, spread blue Butter Cream over top and sides of blue sections, yellow over top and sides of yellow sections and pink over top and sides of pink sections. Spread orange Butter Cream over whistle end and spread plain over remaining sections.

FINISHING TOUCHES

1   Cover top and sides of blue sections with blue candy sprinkles, yellow sections with yellow candy sprinkles and pink sections with pink candy sprinkles. Cover top and sides of cream sections with multi-colored sprinkles.

2   Spoon purple Butter Cream into a pastry bag fitted with a writing tube and pipe in lines between sections and whistle end.

3   Position feathers in center of whistle.

RACING EIGHT

For cake construction see page 209.

STEP-BY-STEP FROSTING

1 Color fondant black. Roll out fondant thinly and place on top of cake. Trim fondant to cake size. Cut 9 of the licorice twists into 2 in/5 cm pieces. Using a little Butter Cream, position licorice pieces around the sides of cake.

2 Spoon Butter Cream into a pastry bag fitted with a star tube and pipe between licorice pieces on sides of cake.

3 Spoon a small quantity of Butter Cream into a pastry bag fitted with a writing tube and pipe in road markings.

4 Cut remaining two licorice twists into ⅛ in/3 mm pieces. Position around inside edges of cake as shown in picture.

FINISHING TOUCHES

Position flags, candles and cycles as shown in picture.

2 x 8¾ in/22 cm ring cakes

8 oz/250 g Covering Fondant (see page 223)

food coloring, black

11 licorice twists

½ quantity Butter Cream (see page 222)

2 black-and-white flags

2 candles

toy motorcycles

From left: Wonderful One (page 202), Sweet Seven (page 205), Fencing Four (page 205), Whistling Six, Racing Eight

CUTTING NUMBER CAKES

The secret to making number cakes is in the cutting.
Use this easy-to-follow number-cutting guide to make number cakes
for people of any age. The general instructions for each are the same. Trim
the tops of cakes so that all cakes to be used for the one number are
the same depth. Use the pictures to cut the cakes to the correct shape
and size. Place the cut cakes upside down on a board and assemble
as shown. Join pieces using a little frosting, then decorate.

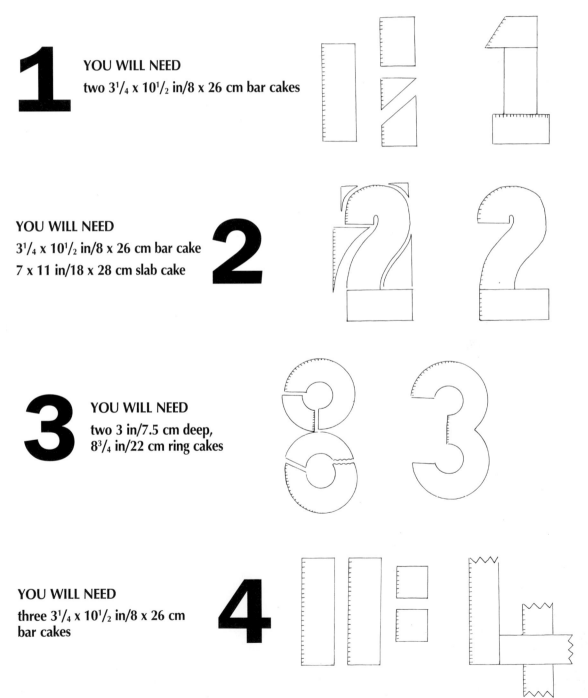

1

YOU WILL NEED
two 3¹/₄ x 10¹/₂ in/8 x 26 cm bar cakes

2

YOU WILL NEED
3¹/₄ x 10¹/₂ in/8 x 26 cm bar cake
7 x 11 in/18 x 28 cm slab cake

3

YOU WILL NEED
two 3 in/7.5 cm deep,
8³/₄ in/22 cm ring cakes

4

YOU WILL NEED
three 3¹/₄ x 10¹/₂ in/8 x 26 cm
bar cakes

5

YOU WILL NEED

$3^1/_4$ x $10^1/_2$ in/8 x 26 cm bar cake

3 in/7.5 cm deep, $8^3/_4$ in/22 cm ring cake

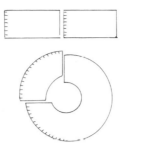
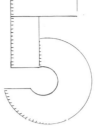

YOU WILL NEED

$3^1/_4$ x $10^1/_2$ in/8 x 26 cm bar cake

3 in/7.5 cm deep, $8^3/_4$ in/22 cm ring cake

(This cake is turned upside down for use as a 9)

6

7

YOU WILL NEED

two $3^1/_4$ x $10^1/_2$ in/8 x 26 cm bar cakes

YOU WILL NEED

two 3 in/7.5 cm deep, $8^3/_4$ in/22 cm ring cakes

8

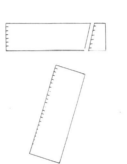
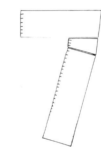

10

YOU WILL NEED

two $3^1/_4$ x $10^1/_2$ in/8 x 26 cm bar cakes

3 in/7.5 cm deep, $8^3/_4$ in/22 cm ring cake

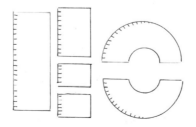
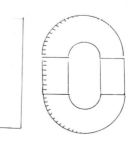

Happy Birthday Cake

Alphabet template (see page 232)
1 x 9 in/23 cm deep round cake
1 quantity Butter Cream (see page 222)
food colorings; pink, blue
long thin pink and blue candles

Trace required letters for message and adjust size (see page 226). Position letter templates on cake and using a skewer prick through the templates to mark message on cake.

STEP-BY-STEP FROSTING

1   Color 6 oz/185 g Butter Cream pink. Color remaining Butter Cream blue.

2   Spoon blue Butter Cream into a pastry bag fitted with a star tube and pipe stars around message outline. Pipe remaining surface of cake with stars.

3   Spoon pink Butter Cream into a pastry bag fitted with a star tube and pipe stars to fill message area.

FINISHING TOUCHES

Using picture as a guide, position candles in the center of the cake.

HOORAY HOORAY CAKE

Trace required letters and numbers for message and adjust size (see page 226). Enlarge the number to stand 4 in/10 cm high.

CAKE CONSTRUCTION

1 Make up Gingerbread Dough according to the recipe. Roll out thinly to $^1/_8$ in/3 mm thickness. Place letter and number templates over dough and using a sharp knife, cut around templates. Cut an extra piece of gingerbread 1 x 4 in/ 2.5 x 10 cm, to act as a support for the number.

2 Place gingerbread shapes on a baking sheet and bake at 400°F/200°C for 15-20 minutes or until golden. Allow gingerbread to stand on sheet for 5 minutes before removing to a wire rack to cool.

3 Trim base of cake and turn upside down on a board. Reserve any cake trimmings.

STEP-BY-STEP FROSTING

1 Color 4 oz/125 g Butter Cream green and 4 oz/125 g purple. Color remaining Butter Cream yellow.

2 Lay gingerbread letters on a flat surface in the order that they will appear on the cake. Using the picture as a guide, frost every alternate letter with green Butter Cream. Frost remaining letters with purple Butter Cream.

3 Using a skewer and the picture as a guide, mark in separation between purple and green colors on the number. Frost one half of the number purple and other half green.

4 Spoon yellow Butter Cream into a pastry bag fitted with a writing tube and pipe outline around each letter.

5 Using picture as a guide, pipe yellow Butter Cream features onto the number.

6 Place reserved cake trimmings in the center of the ring cake to act as a support for the number. Color Fluffy Frosting pale yellow and spread over top and sides of ring cake. Spread some Fluffy Frosting over cake trimmings in center of ring cake.

FINISHING TOUCHES

1 Using picture as a guide, position words on cake.

2 Position number in the center of the cake and use the 1 x 4 in/2.5 x 10 cm piece of gingerbread to support and hold it in place.

Alphabet template (see page 233)

1 x 8$^3/_4$ in/22 cm ring cake

ingredients for $^1/_2$ quantity Gingerbread Dough (see page 182)

1 quantity Fluffy Frosting (see page 222)

$^1/_2$ quantity Butter Cream (see page 222)

food colorings; green, purple, yellow

UR6 Cake (page 215)

Fred the Dog (page 214)

FRED THE DOG

1½ jelly rolls

3 jam rollettes

6 wooden skewers

1 quantity Butter Cream (see page 222)

food colorings; black, orange, brown

1 cup/90 g shredded dry coconut

3 dark brown candy-coated chocolates

1 pink ice cream wafer

30 in/50 cm length, ½ in/1 cm wide tartan ribbon

No template is required to make Fred.

CAKE CONSTRUCTION

1 Place one jelly roll lengthwise on a cutting board. With a sharp knife, round off one end to form rear of body. Starting about one-quarter of the way down the roll, slice an angle from the top down to form breast of dog and base of neck. Round off breast area.

2 To form head, place half jelly roll on cutting board and starting from top, with a sharp knife held at an angle, slice diagonally two sections of roll to form base for ears. Cut out two hollow areas on front of roll to form eye sockets. Holding knife at an angle and starting about three-quarters of the way down the face, cut a slice to form mouth and chin area. Ensure that base of head is rounded to fit angle of neck base. Push wooden skewer through top of head and secure to body.

3 Using two jam rollettes, cut four 1 in/2.5 cm rounds for Fred's feet and two ½ in/1 cm rounds for ears. Taper remaining jam rollette to form tail. Position feet on cake board, secure to body, using Butter Cream. Position ears onto angled side of head with wooden toothpicks. Push wooden skewers through tail into body to secure.

STEP-BY-STEP FROSTING

1 Color 2 oz/60 g Butter Cream black. Color remaining Butter Cream rust brown using orange and brown food colorings.

2 Spread rust brown Butter Cream liberally over Fred, ensuring that his shape is retained.

3 Color coconut brown and, using your hands, carefully press all over Fred.

FINISHING TOUCHES

1 Using picture as a guide, position brown candy-coated chocolates for eyes and nose. Cut pink wafer to form Fred's tongue and position.

2 Tie tartan ribbon around Fred's neck.

UR6 CAKE

No template is required to make the rocket.

CAKE CONSTRUCTION

1 Cut one end of half jelly roll to form a V. This will be the front of the rocket.

2 Cut one jam rollette in half. These will be the rocket's exhausts.

3 Cut remaining two jam rollettes at an angle at one end so they will sit against the body of the rocket as wings.

4 Join jelly rolls using a little Butter Cream. Using picture as a guide, position rocket wings and exhausts, holding these in place with wooden skewers and a little Butter Cream. Place assembled cake on a board.

STEP-BY-STEP FROSTING

1 Color 4 oz/125 g Butter Cream red. Leave remaining Butter Cream plain.

2 Using picture as a guide and a skewer, mark in rocket markings.

3 Spoon plain Butter Cream into a pastry bag fitted with star tube and outline areas that will be red, with stars. Cover remaining body and wings of rocket with stars.

4 Spoon red Butter Cream into a pastry bag fitted with a star tube and fill the remaining areas with red stars. Cover rocket exhausts with red stars.

1¹/₂ jelly rolls

3 jam rollettes

1 quantity Butter Cream (see page 222)

food coloring, red

THE BASICS

In this chapter you will
find a Basic Butter Cake recipe
that makes a great base for the birthday
cakes, frosting recipes, decorating
techniques and the templates for
the birthday cakes. You will also find
hints and tips on successful cake baking
and much more.

Basic Butter Cake with variations (page 218)

BASIC BUTTER CAKE

½ cup/1 stick/125 g butter or shortening

1 teaspoon vanilla

¾ cup/170 g superfine sugar

2 eggs

1½ cups/185 g flour, sifted

1½ teaspoons baking powder

½ cup/125 mL milk

1   Place butter or shortening and vanilla in a bowl and beat until light and fluffy. Gradually add sugar, beating well until creamy.

2   Add eggs one at a time, beating well after each addition. Sift flour and baking powder together. Fold flour mixture and milk, alternately, into butter mixture.

3   Spoon batter into a prepared cake pan and bake according to size of pan you have chosen (see Cooking Chart for Butter Cake opposite). Stand in pan for 5 minutes before turning onto a wire rack to cool. When cold, top with frosting of your choice.

Chocolate Cake: Mix 2 oz/60 g melted cooled chocolate into the basic cake mixture before adding flour mixture and milk. Replace 2 tablespoons flour with 2 tablespoons cocoa powder. Bake according to pan size you have chosen.

Apple Cake: Spread two-thirds of the cake mixture into a prepared cake pan. Top with ¾ cup/185 g cold stewed apple, then remaining cake mixture. Bake according to pan size you have chosen. Allow cake to stand in pan for 10 minutes before turning onto a wire rack to cool.

Orange Cake: Replace vanilla with 2 teaspoons finely grated orange rind. Replace ⅓ cup/90 mL milk with ⅓ cup/ 90 mL orange juice. Bake according to pan size you have chosen.

Coffee Cake: Replace vanilla with 1 tablespoon instant coffee powder dissolved in 1 tablespoon boiling water. Cool before adding to butter. Bake according to pan size you have chosen.

Coconut Cake: Replace vanilla with ½ teaspoon coconut extract (optional) and add ½ cup/45 g grated dry coconut to flour mixture. Bake according to pan size you have chosen.

Banana Cake: Omit milk from recipe. Add 3 small ripe mashed bananas to the butter and egg mixture. Sift together flour, baking powder and 1 teaspoon baking soda and fold into banana mixture. Bake according to pan size you have chosen.

COOKING CHART FOR BUTTER CAKE

Pan Size	Type	Mixture Quantity	Oven Temp °F	Oven Temp °C	Cooking Time
3 in/7.5 cm deep, 7 in/18 cm	round	1	350	180	40-45 mins
3 in/7.5 cm deep, 8 in/20 cm	round	1	350	180	45 mins
3 in/7.5 cm deep, 9 in/23 cm	round	1½	350	180	50-55 mins
3 in/7.5 cm deep, 7 in/18 cm	square	1	350	180	45-50 mins
3 in/7.5 cm deep, 8 in/20 cm	square	1	350	180	40-45 mins
3 in/7.5 cm deep, 9 in/23 cm	square	2	350	180	50-55 mins
3 in/7.5 cm deep, 9 in/23 cm	straight-sided ring or tube	1	350	180	35-40 mins
3¼ x 10½ in/8 x 26 cm	bar	½	350	180	30-35 mins
7 x 11¼ in/18 x 28 cm	slab	1	350	180	30-35 mins
4½ x 8½ in/11 x 21 cm	loaf	1	350	180	60 mins
5 cup/1.25 liter	round-bottomed ovenproof basin	1	350	180	1¼ hours
7 cup/1.75 liter	round-bottomed ovenproof basin	1	350	180	1¾ hours

BASIC SPONGE CAKE

4 eggs

1 cup/250 g superfine sugar

1¼ cups/155 g self-rising flour, sifted

½ cup/125 mL milk, warmed

2 teaspoons melted butter

1   Place eggs in a large bowl and beat until light and fluffy. Add sugar a little at a time, beating well after each addition. Continue beating until mixture is very thick and creamy.

2   Fold flour into egg mixture. Combine milk and butter and fold into egg mixture. Pour batter into a greased and floured cake pan and bake according to size of pan you have chosen.

COOKING CHART FOR SPONGE CAKE

Pan Size (all 1½ in/4 cm deep)	Type	Mixture Quantity	Oven Temp °F	Oven Temp °C	Cooking Time
7 in/18 cm	round layer	½	350	180	20 mins
8 in/20 cm	round layer	½	350	180	25 mins
10½ x 12¾ in/26 x 32 cm	jelly roll	1	350	180	20 mins
7 x 11¼ in/18 x 28 cm	slab	1	350	180	30 mins

VANILLA BUTTER FROSTING

Place confectioners' sugar and butter in a bowl, add boiling water and mix to make a frosting of an easy-to-spread consistency, adding a little more water if necessary. Beat in vanilla and food coloring, if using.

Chocolate Butter Frosting: Add ¼ cup/30 g cocoa powder to boiling water.

Coffee Butter Frosting: Add 1 tablespoon instant coffee powder to boiling water.

Lemon Butter Frosting: Replace vanilla with 1-2 teaspoons lemon juice.

Passion Fruit Frosting: Replace vanilla with 2-3 tablespoons passion fruit pulp. A little more confectioners' sugar may be required to make a frosting of spreadable consistency.

Makes enough to cover an 8 in/20 cm cake or 18 cookies

1½ cups/230 g confectioners' sugar, sifted

¼ cup/½ stick/60 g butter

2 tablespoons boiling water

¼ teaspoon vanilla

few drops food coloring (optional)

BUTTER CREAM

1 cup/2 sticks/250 g butter
1 lb/500 g confectioners' sugar
¹/₄ cup/60 mL milk

1   Place butter in a bowl and beat until light and creamy.

2   Add confectioners' sugar and milk and continue to beat until smooth.

FLUFFY FROSTING

¹/₂ cup/125 mL water
1¹/₄ cups/315 g sugar
3 egg whites

1   Place water and sugar in a saucepan and cook, over a medium heat, stirring constantly without boiling, until sugar dissolves. Brush any sugar from sides of pan using a pastry brush dipped in water.

2   Bring syrup to the boil and boil rapidly, without stirring, for 3-5 minutes or until syrup reaches the soft-ball stage (239°F/115°C on a candy thermometer).

3   Place egg whites in a large bowl and beat until soft peaks form. Continue beating while pouring in syrup in a thin stream a little at a time. Continue beating until all the syrup is used and frosting will stand in stiff peaks.

MARSHMALLOW FROSTING

Makes enough to fill and cover an 8 in/ 20 cm cake

1 egg white
2 teaspoons gelatin dissolved in ¹/₂ cup/ 125 mL hot water, cooled
1 cup/155 g confectioners' sugar
flavoring of your choice
few drops of food coloring (optional)

Place egg white in a bowl and beat until soft peaks form, then continue beating while gradually adding gelatin mixture. Beat in confectioners' sugar, flavoring and coloring, if using. Continue beating until frosting is thick.

ROYAL ICING

1   Place egg white in a bowl and beat with a wooden spoon.

2   Add confectioners' sugar 1 tablespoon at a time, beating well after each addition. When icing reaches piping consistency, stir in a few drops of lemon juice.

1 egg white

1½ cups/250 g confectioners' sugar

a little lemon juice

CHOCOLATE FUDGE FROSTING

1   Place sugar and evaporated milk in a heavy-based saucepan and cook over a low heat, stirring, until sugar dissolves. Bring mixture to the boil and simmer, stirring constantly, for 4 minutes.

2   Remove pan from heat and stir in chocolate. Continue stirring until chocolate melts, then stir in butter and vanilla.

3   Transfer frosting to a bowl and set aside to cool. Cover with plastic wrap and chill until frosting thickens and is of a spreadable consistency.

Makes enough to fill and cover an 8 in/ 20 cm cake

¾ cup/170 g superfine sugar

⅓ cup/90 mL evaporated milk

4 oz/125 g semi-sweet cooking chocolate, broken into pieces

3 tablespoons/45 g butter

¼ teaspoon vanilla

COVERING FONDANT

1   Place water in top of double boiler. Sprinkle over gelatin, stir and set aside to stand for 10 minutes.

2   Place bowl over a saucepan of simmering water and heat, stirring constantly, until gelatin dissolves. Add corn syrup and mix well. Remove bowl from heat and set aside to cool slightly.

3   Place 1½ lb/750 g confectioners' sugar in a large bowl. Make a well in the center and pour in gelatin mixture. Stir, drawing sugar from the sides until a firm paste forms. Turn paste onto a surface lightly dusted with confectioners' sugar and knead until smooth and pliable. Place fondant in a plastic bag, seal and leave at room temperature for at least 24 hours.

4   Turn paste onto a surface lightly dusted with confectioners' sugar and knead in remaining sugar. Use as directed in birthday cake recipes.

This amount of fondant will cover an 8 in/ 20 cm round or square cake

3 tablespoons cold water

1 tablespoon unflavored gelatin

½ cup/125 mL light corn syrup

2 lb/1 kg confectioners' sugar, sifted

DECORATING ESSENTIALS

Before you start to frost or decorate a cake, place cake on a thick piece of cardboard, cut to fit. When making a fancy shaped cake, use the paper template to cut a heavy cardboard base the same size and shape as the cake. Cover with foil and place the cut-out cake on it. When you have frosted your cake, allow the frosting to set before transferring to a serving board. To transfer cake to serving board, slip a wide spatula under the board and you will find that the cake can be moved easily without fear of damage to cake.

FROSTINGS
Correct frosting consistency is the key to successful cake decorating. Different consistencies of frostings are required depending on the decorations and type of frosting being used.

Stiff—the frosting can peak to an inch or more.

Medium — a peak of less than an inch.

Thin — the frosting flows easily from a tube when a pastry bag is squeezed.

COLORINGS
Various types of food colorings are available — water-soluble powders, pastes and liquids. All of these can be used to color Butter Cream or Royal Icing. Care should be taken not to overmix when adding coloring to Fluffy Frosting, as volume will drop and frosting will become too thin to apply to the cake.

To color the frosting: Tint a small amount of frosting first, then mix into remaining white frosting.

Use an eye dropper to add coloring and add a drop at a time. Remember you can always add more color, but it is much more difficult to lighten a frosting. Even when a very dark frosting is required the coloring should still be added gradually.

Always ensure that you have colored enough frosting to frost and decorate the whole cake as it is very hard to reproduce the exact color.

Take care when working with food coloring as it will stain hands, clothes and work surfaces. It should, however, wash away with soap or detergent.

PASTRY BAGS
Nylon pastry bags are probably the simplest to use. They come in several sizes and are available from cake decorating suppliers and department stores. You can make your own paper pastry bag from waxed paper. Paper pastry bags are easy to make and inexpensive. They are particularly useful when decorating a cake with a number of different colors or when only a small quantity of frosting is used. Paper pastry bags are fragile however and with a large amount of frosting inside, the paper may split because of the pressure of the contents and the heat and moisture of your hands. Use nylon pastry bags for larger areas.

MAKING A PAPER PASTRY BAG

1 Cut a 10 in/25 cm square of waxed paper.

2 Cut square in half diagonally to form two triangles.

3 To make pastry bag, place paper triangles on top of each other and mark the three corners A, B and C.

4 Fold corner B around and inside corner A.

5 Bring corner C around the outside of the bag until it fits exactly behind corner A. At this stage all three corners should be together and point closed.

6 Fold corner A over two or three times to hold the bag together.

7 Snip the point off the bag and drop in frosting tube. The pastry bag can also be used without a tube for writing and outlines, in which case only the very tip of the point should be snipped off the bag.

To fill the pastry bag: Spoon the frosting into the bag to half fill. Fold the top over about ½ in/1 cm then fold over again. Fold the tips towards the center and press with your thumb on the join to force the frosting out.

Holding the pastry bag: To hold the pastry bag correctly, grip the bag near the top with the folded or twisted end held between the thumb and fingers. Guide the bag with your free hand. Right-handed people should decorate from left to right, while left-handers will decorate from right to left, the exception being when piping writing.

The final appearance of your decorated cake will be directly affected by how you squeeze and relax your grip on the pastry bag, that is, the pressure that you apply and the steadiness of that pressure. The pressure should be so consistent that you can move the bag in a free-and-easy glide with just the right amount of frosting flowing from the tube. A little practice will soon have you feeling confident.

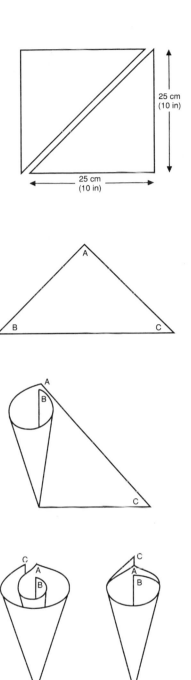

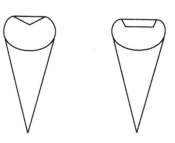

CHOCOLATE DECORATIONS

CHOCOLATE SHAVINGS
These can be made by running a vegetable peeler down the side of a block of chocolate. If the chocolate is cold you will get shavings, if at room temperature, the shavings will curl.

CHOCOLATE CURLS (CARAQUES)
These are made by spreading a layer of melted chocolate over a marble, granite or ceramic work surface. Allow the chocolate to set at room temperature. Then, holding a metal pastry scraper or large knife at a 45° angle slowly push it along the work surface away from you to form chocolate into cylinders. If chocolate shavings form, then it is too cold and it is best to start again.

ENLARGING TEMPLATES

The templates used in this book have been reduced to fit the pages. They have been drawn on a squared grid where each square is 1 in/2.5 cm. The easiest way to size a template is to reduce or enlarge it on a photocopier. Alternatively, to enlarge the templates to their actual size follow these simple steps:

1   On a piece of firm paper, draw a grid with each square measuring 1 x 1 in/2.5 x 2.5 cm. Tape a piece of waxed or parchment paper over the grid. Drawing the template on paper in this way will enable you to re-use the grid again and again.

2   With a sharp, soft pencil begin drawing at a point where the template line coincides with the intersection of four squares. Make a dot at this point.

3   Work your way carefully around the template piece making a dot at each point where the template line intersects with a line of the grid.

4   Now simply join the dots. Keep a soft eraser handy for any little slips or squiggles.

5   Cut out the template and label if necessary.

It is a good idea also to make a board to sit the cake on at the same time as you are making the template. Cut a heavy piece of cardboard the same size and shape as the template.

USING ALPHABETS

The following easy instructions will ensure that your message looks just as you want it on your cake.

1   Choose the alphabet you wish to use and check that it is the right size for the cake. The easiest way to change the size of the alphabet is to enlarge or reduce it on a photocopier.

2   Using a ruler, draw a straight line on a piece of tracing paper.

3   Place the tracing paper over the lettering style of your choice, aligning the straight line with the base or the first letter of your word.

4   Carefully trace the letter. Move the tracing paper and re-align the straight line and trace the next letter. Continue in this way until you have the complete word. For a multi-worded message use a separate sheet of tracing paper for each word.

5   Draw the size and shape of your cake top on a piece of paper and arrange the traced words in a suitable balanced layout, remembering to take into account any other decorations you will have on top of the cake.

6   When you are happy with your layout, join the separate pieces of paper together with Scotch tape. Now make a new tracing on a clean piece of tracing paper. This will be your template.

7   Place the template on cake top and using a fine skewer or thick needle, pinprick a dotted line through the message onto your cake top. This line will be your piping guide line.

8   Spoon frosting into a pastry bag fitted with a writing tube and pipe in message using the dotted line as your guide.

SPUN SUGAR

1   Place sugar, water and cream of tartar in a small saucepan and heat over a low heat, stirring constantly, until sugar dissolves.

2   Increase heat and bring syrup to the boil, without stirring. Boil until syrup is golden. Brush any sugar from sides of pan using a pastry brush dipped in water.

3   Remove pan from heat and set aside to cool slightly.

4   Coat the back of two wooden spoons with toffee, place them back to back and gently pull apart. As a thread of toffee forms, continue pulling apart until the toffee starts to set and threads have formed.

5   Place toffee thread over cake or dessert. Repeat until all the toffee is used.

1 cup/250 g sugar

¹/₂ cup/125 mL water

pinch cream of tartar

FROSTED FRUIT

Frosted strawberries, cherries, small bunches of grapes or redcurrants make wonderful decorations for cold desserts and cakes.

To frost fruit: Rinse fruit and drain well on paper towels. Break into small bunches or single pieces and remove any leaves or unwanted stems. Place an egg white in a small bowl and whisk lightly. Dip fruit in egg white. Remove, set aside to drain slightly, then coat with superfine sugar. Stand on a wire rack to dry for 2 hours or until set. Frosted fruit is best used on the day you do it, but will keep for 12 hours in an airtight container.

You can also crystallize miniature roses, rose petals and mint leaves using this method.

fruit of your choice

1 egg white

superfine sugar

TOFFEE FRUIT

1   Place sugar and water in a small saucepan and heat over a low heat, stirring constantly, until sugar dissolves.

2   Increase heat and bring syrup to the boil, without stirring. Boil for 8 minutes or until syrup is thick. Brush any sugar from sides of pan using a pastry brush dipped in water.

3   Remove pan from heat and stand in a sink of cold water for 2 minutes. Dip fruit in toffee to coat completely, allow excess toffee to drain from fruit and place on a greased wire rack to set.

1 cup/250 g sugar

²/₃ cup/170 mL water

fruit of your choice, cleaned

TEMPLATE - LEO THE LION   Each square is equal to 1 in x 1 in (2.5 cm x 2.5 cm)

TEMPLATE - SOLDIER BOY   Each square is equal to 1 in x 1 in (2.5 cm x 2.5 cm)

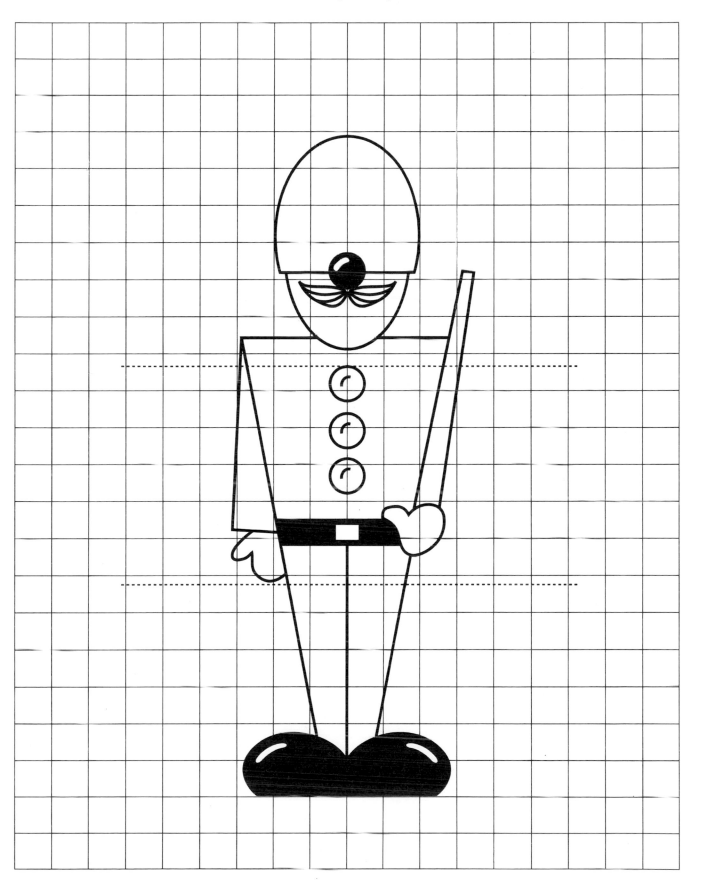

TEMPLATE - COLA BOTTLE   Each square is equal to 1 in x 1 in (2.5 cm x 2.5 cm)

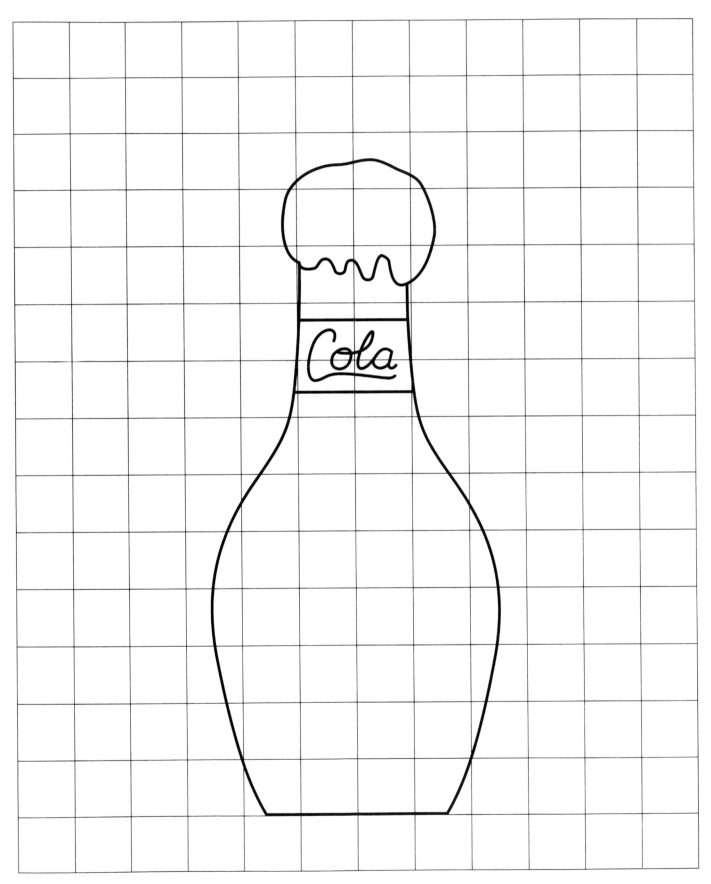

TEMPLATE - GINGERBREAD MAN   Each square is equal to 1 in x 1 in (2.5 cm x 2.5 cm)

ABCDEFGHIJK
LMNOPQRSTU
VWXYZ

a b c d e f g h i j k l m n

o p q r s t u v w x y z

ABCDEFGHIJ
KLMNOPQR
STUVWXYZ

abcdefghijklmno

pqrstuvwxyz

BAKING SECRETS

What happens when you make a cake? One of the secrets to producing wonderful cakes and cookies is to understand why certain techniques are used.

MAKING THE CAKE

Many recipes begin by creaming the butter and sugar. This is an important process as little bubbles of air are trapped in the mixture and it is this air which helps to produce a light-textured cake.

The butter should be softened for the creaming process and the mixture beaten until it is creamy and fluffy and almost doubled in volume.

Creaming can be done with a balloon whisk, wooden spoon, electric mixer or food processor.

After the creaming process, an egg or eggs are often added to the mixture. The egg white forms a layer around each bubble of air and as the cake cooks the egg white coagulates and forms a wall around each bubble, preventing the bubbles from bursting and so ruining the cake.

As the cake cooks, the air bubbles expand and the cake rises.

As the air bubbles are expanding, the gluten in the flour is also stretching. This will continue until the gluten loses its elasticity.

Do not open the oven door until at least halfway through the recommended cooking time or the rising process is interrupted. With the sudden drop in temperature the cake stops expanding and it sinks because there is no structure to support it.

The oven should be preheated to the correct temperature before placing the cake in to bake.

If baking more than one cake, arrange the pans so that they do not touch each other or the sides of the oven.

Filling the cake pan is an important step towards a successful result. If your batter is soft it can be poured into the cake pan, however a firm batter should be spooned into the pan and spread out evenly using a spatula. For light batters, only half to two-thirds fill the pan; heavy batters can fill as much as three-quarters of the pan.

IS THE CAKE COOKED?

Test your cake just before the end of the cooking. To test the cake, insert a skewer into the thickest part of the cake. If it comes away clean, your cake is cooked. If there is still cake mixture on the skewer, cook for 5 minutes longer then test again.

Alternatively, you can gently press the top of the cake with your fingertips. When cooked the depression will spring back quickly.

When the cake starts to leave the sides of the pan is another indication that the cake is cooked.

COOLING THE CAKE

You will find that a freshly baked cake is very fragile. Allow a cake to stand for a short time in the pan before turning onto a wire rack to cool.

Before turning out a cake, loosen the sides with a spatula or palette knife. Turn the cake onto a wire rack, then immediately invert onto a second wire rack so that the top of the cake is not marked with indentations from the rack. If you do not have a second wire rack, invert the cake onto a clean cloth on your hand then turn it back onto the wire rack.

STORING BAKED GOODS

Allow cakes to cool completely before placing in an airtight container, or condensation will accumulate in the container and cause the cake to go moldy.

Keeping times for cakes vary depending on the ingredients used. A fatless sponge will only stay fresh for 1-2 days while one made with fat will keep fresh for 3 days. Cakes made using the creaming method usually keep fresh for up to a week. Light fruit cakes keep for 2-3 weeks and heavy rich fruit cakes will store for a month or more.

Most undecorated cakes can be frozen successfully. Wrap the cake in freezer wrap or place in a freezer bag and seal. If freezing several cakes, wrap each separately or place freezer wrap or waxed paper between cakes so that they are easy to remove.

To thaw a frozen cake, leave in package and thaw at room temperature. Large cakes will take 3-4 hours to thaw, layer cakes 1-2 hours and small cakes about 30 minutes.

PREPARING THE CAKE PANS

To grease and flour a cake pan: Using a pastry brush lightly brush cake pan with melted butter or margarine, then sprinkle with flour and shake to coat evenly. Invert pan on work surface and tap gently to remove excess flour.

To grease and line a round cake pan: Place cake pan on a large piece of parchment paper and using a pencil trace around the base, then cut out shape. Grease pan and line with paper.

To line a deep cake pan: A deep cake pan should be lined on the bottom and sides. Use a double-thickness folded strip of parchment paper 2 in/5 cm higher than the cake pan and long enough to fit around the pan and to overlap by about 1 in/2.5 cm. On the folded edge turn up about 1 in/2.5 cm and crease, then using scissors snip at regular intervals across the margin as far as the fold. Cut out a piece of parchment paper to line the bottom of the pan as described previously. Grease the pan and place the strip inside the pan with the snipped margin lying flat on the bottom of the pan. Ensure that the ends overlap so that the sides are completely covered by the paper. Place the bottom piece of parchment paper in the pan to cover the snipped margin.

To line a loaf pan: Cut a strip of parchment paper the width of the bottom of the pan and long enough to come up the shorter sides of the pan and overlap by 1 in/2.5 cm. Grease the pan and line with the paper. When the cake is cooked the unlined sides can be loosened with a knife and the paper ends are used to lift out the cake.

INDEX